T

The Secret Diary
of
St Gargoyle's

aged 984 ¾

Ron Wood

CANTERBURY
PRESS
Norwich

Text and illustrations © Ron Wood 2003

First published in 2003 by the Canterbury Press Norwich
(a publishing imprint of Hymns Ancient & Modern
Limited, a registered charity)
St Mary's Works, St Mary's Plain,
Norwich, Norfolk NR3 3BH

www.scm-canterburypress.co.uk

British Library Cataloguing in Publication data

A catalogue record for this book is available
from the British Library

ISBN 1-85311-537-1

Typeset by Regent Typesetting, London
Printed and bound by
Bookmarque, Croydon, Surrey

January

1st January, Monday

What a way to start the year, with what appears to be a dose of flu. Throat like a churchyard path, head banging like a TV evangelist, and very uncharitable of Hilary to say I've got a hangover.

Snowdrop out in the churchyard. A little white head nodding among the gravestones. I phoned Ray and Dennis. They arrived with a rope, a net, and what looked like a tree stake, which was a little unnecessary if you ask me. But Snowdrop led them a merry chase over most of God's little acre, then put up a mighty struggle when cornered, and there were artificial flowers everywhere by the time she was in the back of the van. Ray called, 'Thank you, Vicar' as they roared off, and added out of the window that the angel's ear will probably go back on with superglue.

2nd January, Tuesday

The gravedigger busy all day in the frozen churchyard. In the permafrost layer, he found the body of a mammoth in a good state of preservation. He says not to worry, that green astroturf stuff the undertakers use will cover it up.

Visited the Bloats in Ferrets' Bottom, picking my way past the burnt-out cars to the house with the Police Aware sticker on it. Small Bloats were everywhere, biting my ankles and eating the food in the dog's bowl. I suspect Shane is deliberately trying to have as many children as possible so that one day

they will outnumber the Orrells. I reminded them that I do baptisms as part of the job. Shane Bloat's cigarette bobbed about as he said, 'That's the one with the water, isn't it?' I said it was, and he sucked in his breath so hard his cigarette shrank visibly, even though it wasn't lit.

Hangover nearly gone.

3rd January, Wednesday
The boys say they're going to clone a mammoth for their school science project, using one of their rabbits to gestate the foetus they will create. I hope I was able to sound encouraging without being patronizing.

Poor turnout at the midweek service, and I could see my breath in clouds. Afraid someone might get the chalice stuck to their bottom lip, and wondered what the theological implications might be. Colonel

Toop said I should have served it chambréed and I said I had. Room temperature just happened to be zero degrees. Hilary put on her woollen hat with the earflaps and dug around in the freezer so we had meat pie for supper. I don't care what meat it was. It wasn't turkey, and that's the important thing.

4th January, Thursday
Funeral of old Joe Blake, aged 96, who always said he wanted to die by being shot by a jealous lover. Unfortunately, he died of nothing in particular in his sleep the day after Boxing Day, leaving the jealous lover frustrated, and gnashing her gums. Funeral arrangements conducted in their usual incompetent way by the Dolts. As the bearers staggered across the frosted grass, I thought they would drop the coffin. They looked like Joe's schoolmates. Reaching the grave, Henry Dolt told them for some reason to turn the coffin round, so the thick end of the coffin became wedged in the thin end of the grave. Henry joined in the ensuing tugging, and Joe had a white knuckle ride until the coffin came up again, covered with thick brown fur. Most of this fell off as they turned it round again, and Joe was finally laid to his rest, which I felt he'd earned. Henry Dolt said afterwards, 'I thought that didn't go off too badly', which by his standards is probably true.

5th January, Friday

No jobs worth pursuing in *Church Times* unless I want to be vicar of 14 parishes in Lincolnshire. Trying to make it sound tempting, they point out that it's nice and flat for riding a bike. I love the way they always say, 'Are you the person we're looking for?' as if they were expecting 44,000 applications.

Angry scenes and confrontations because the boys accused Hilary of throwing away their science project. She insisted she'd never seen it and didn't know anything about it, but they were not to be placated, because they go back to school on Monday, and where were they going to find another frozen mammoth before then?

After lunch, I drove over to Bishop's Wibbling to borrow a thurible. Keith pointed over my shoulder and said, 'Greetings, Father Ron', because he always does, and laughed like an idiot. He's so high only bats can hear him preach, and when I said what I wanted, he asked which one, and showed me in the vestry where he keeps several. How many priests, I asked myself, have several thuribles? I chose the one with the least curly bits on, some of those little charcoal things and a heaped spoonful of what looked like those poncey sugar crystals they put out at dinner parties. Keith stuck his nose in the bag, took a deep sniff, and came out even higher. I thanked him and left, and I swear he was humming 'Golden Brown'.

6th January, Epiphany

But we're doing a special service tomorrow. If we'd had a service today nobody would have come because it snowed hard all afternoon. Hilary took the boys off to town on the bus, shopping, leaving me to finish my sermon, and try to work out what the blank you do with a thurible. Why didn't I do my theology in Chichester? They'd have taught me how to work one there, instead of filling my head with all that nonsense about ethics.

The first tramp of the year called. Once I'd established he wasn't God in disguise, and had, in fact, no pretensions to deity at all, I gave him the rest of the meat pie microwaved, a thick cheese-and-pickle sandwich and a mug of hot tea.

Hilary came back from the shops laden with carrier bags full of her loot from the sales. I don't want to know what it all cost, and I still don't see how spending on such a heroic scale saves money. The boys had spent some of their Christmas money on Action Man Evangelical, with Actual Clapping

Hands, and a John the Baptist whose head really comes off. It was cheap, they said, because the platter was missing, and they spent a happy time making one out of the foil dish from a mince pie.

7th January, First Sunday of Epiphany

Snow. The service went well up to a point. The crib had been left in church for an extra day, and if the boys think I didn't notice one of the shepherds had been replaced by an Action Man with an AK47, they are mistaken. The procession following the choir was supposed to be: a sidesman with the collection, symbolizing gold; Adrian with the thurible, symbolizing frankincense; and me with the chalice, because I have no idea what myrrh is beyond a symbol of death, and I thought I'd carry the chalice in and let people work it out for themselves.

Apparently, Adrian in the vestry had no more idea than me how to work a thurible. His excuse that he's only a Reader is downright feeble. He couldn't make the charcoal briquettes light, and when he heard me say 'and finally' he realized he had less than a quarter of an hour left. So he resorted to the old barbecue technique, and poured some of the oil we use in the altar candles on it, added the incense and put a match to it. Then he joined me in due course at the back of the church. Everyone started singing 'As with gladness men of old' with what passes for gusto in these parts. As we reached the chancel step, the thurible hit it in full swing, the top came off, and the burning charcoal flew out.

By a coincidence, one of the firemen was Jason Blake, one of Joe's grandsons who'd been at the funeral. Isn't that strange?

8th January, Monday

Day off. Thwarted in my plan to spend it building a giant spaceship out of the boys' Lego, because I had to spend a good hour up in the loft looking for the leak in the roof. A large wet patch had appeared on the carpet of the boys' room. I was set upon by spiders the size of sweeps' brushes, scratched by that hairy stuff they wrap around the water tanks, and hit my head on the rafters more than once. But the roof seems to be quite sound, and there is no sign that the tanks leak.

Hilary said, 'Who's eaten all the mince pies, then?' and we all said it wasn't us, and she said somebody had better, then, because she wasn't making any cake until we did.

9th January, Tuesday

Another morning spent with the sad, the sick and the depressed at the clergy chapter meeting. The assembled vicars and curates all had a sort of dissipated look, and when Barry the rural dean offered mince pies there were no takers. I gave Keith the thurible back. He said, 'Do you realize there are only two firms that can do the sort of repair it needs, and they are both in  Italy?' We had a talk on Marcellus of Ancyra, Champion of the Homoousios with colour slides, which were less interesting than watching

Shirley crossing and uncrossing her legs. So there is something to be said for ordaining women after all.

More tears and confrontations when the boys accused me of stealing their snowman. Hilary backed me up, and suggested he might have run away to hide, and we even offered to help them look for him. We put on coats and wellies to search the garden, while the boys looked under their beds, of all places. What funny little chaps they are.

10th January, Wednesday
Took the boys to school because Hilary was at her class. Their new teacher is a Miss Bracie. As soon as she saw me her face lit up. 'You're a vicar!' she said. The dog collar has always meant I could never get away with pretending to be anything other than a vicar, or (once) a secret agent pretending to be a vicar. So I just said, 'Yes.' 'Only the boys told me you wear dresses,' she said. I shall rewrite my will. Soon.

11th January, Thursday
The new trousers Hilary gave me for Christmas will have to go back. If they're a 34 waist, I'm a Dutchman. Visited old Mrs Hole who complained about her arthritis, tried to demonstrate what she couldn't do because of it and got stuck like it. Phoned Dr Kelly. I could smell his breath over the phone. He said could I bring her down to the surgery, and I said not without slinging her over my

shoulder like a sack, so he said he'd be there as soon
as possible. I made my escape.

12th January, Friday
In a weak moment decided to visit Miss Threadgold
who was in fine form, and said she'd have put on
the black stockings if she'd known I was coming.
She offered me sherry, but I declined as it was only
10 o'clock, and she then accused me of having no
festive spirit, and pointed out the mistletoe. I said it
should have come down last Saturday, but she just
laughed, and said it wasn't coming down until
she'd had her money's worth. While she was in the
bathroom, I made a rope by knotting the bedsheets
together, and made my getaway.

13th January, Saturday
I tried, just for fun, to write a sermon in rhyme. I
once knew a priest who could do it all the time, but
I think that he had lots of time on his hands, or at
least hyperactive poetry glands, because after a few
lines I had to give it best, and write it in prose like
all of the rest.

14th January, Second Sunday of Epiphany
Drove through grey, snowy landscape to Peedle
Magna for early service. Two came, including me.
I'll be glad when they get a new vicar of their own.

Back just in time for service here. Gave them the
one about putting the Christmas festivities behind

us, and looking forward to whatever the New Year brings. When I said we must thank God for whatever he sends us in 1989, they put it down to my waggish sense of humour, which is another thing to thank God for.

15th January, Monday
Tried not to listen to *Thought for the Day* because it's my day off, but tripped over the cat on my way to the radio, and had to lie there, prone, with my chin in the Kit-e-Kat while some rabbi shared his insights with me. It's all right for him. He won't spend the day smelling of fish. Hilary made me clear out the garage so we can keep the car in the warm.

16th January, Tuesday
After a busy morning visiting the sick, the old, and the generally unhappy, I called in at the Temporary Sign for something warming. Doris behind the bar said she didn't think I'd show my face again after New Years' Eve, but then winked and added, 'Never mind – it just shows you're human!'

17th January, Wednesday
I set everything out for the midweek service, and at 10 o'clock there was nobody there. So I blew out the candles, and put everything away, tidy. Came out of the vestry to find a congregation of nine sitting there looking expectant. Set everything up

again, lit the candles and carried on with as much panache as I could muster in freezing conditions. Must get my watch fixed.

18th January, Thursday

School assembly, the first after the Christmas break. Good to see their bright little faces looking  up at me, all shiny with eager anticipation. I told them the story of Tamar and Judah from Genesis 38, and warned them against doing what Onan did. Miss Jolly came up to me afterwards, shaking slightly, said I'd really held their attention, and she still had no idea what it was Onan did. As she has a face like a dog sucking a wasp, she probably never will.

19th January, Friday

Bumped into Dr Kelly in the General Stores. His breath is so bad you can actually see it, and Mrs General covered the cakes with a cloth until he'd gone. He said, 'Good morning Vicar, how are the piles?' which apparently passes for good-humoured banter in his part of Ireland. I said I don't have piles, for the benefit of the ladies in the queue, and he said, 'Maybe you should buy a lottery ticket, then!' which made them all shriek with laughter. Why do I let myself get drawn?

20th January, Saturday

Off to town to take advantage of the sales at Cassocks R Us. Dog collars were buy two, get one free, so I did, and clerical socks were irresistible at the price, so I didn't resist. I reckoned I already have enough CDs of Gregorian chants, but then, gripped by sale fever, I bought a hundred of those little round cards with a hole that stop candles dribbling on your hands, even though I have no idea when they might get used.

21st January, Third Sunday of Epiphany

Up at crack of dawn, leaving Hilary in bed. I remarked that the Gospel today was about how Jesus travelled from place to place, spreading the word, and healing the sick, and doing good. From under the bedclothes came a snort, and the comment, 'And you just travel around.' Thus encouraged, I drove over to Peedle Parva for early service. Nobody came. A game not worth the candle. Or, as it happens, two candles. I hope they get a new vicar soon. Then he can turn out on a cold morning for an empty church. Journey not entirely wasted, as I ran over a pheasant on the way back, and stuck it in the boot.

22nd January, Monday
Day off. Spent it making a giant spaceship out of the boys' Lego.

23rd January, Tuesday
A whole day with nothing in the diary, so I spent it catching up with people I haven't visited for ages, and who were on my conscience. Mrs Trout said, 'Ooh, I thought you must be dead!' with heavy sarcasm, and then told me all about her operation, with vivid sign language. By the time she got around to asking me if I wanted a mince pie with my coffee, the answer was definitely 'No'. I put my foot in it at Mrs Blunder's. Her husband was ill for so long I got quite used to asking how he was. I asked, 'How is Alf?' and she answered, quite calmly, 'Still dead.'

Bible study in the evening at Mrs Jellicle's. The group has decided to study the minor prophets this year, what with there being 12 of them. So we started with Hosea, who learned of God's love and forgiveness through the unfaithfulness of his wife. Not a dry eye in the house. Mrs Jellicle offered us mince pies and was surprised there were no takers. Her husband had decamped to the Temporary Sign for the evening on the grounds that he is an atheist. Mrs Jellicle said, 'It's such a shame. He came from a very religious family, did Evan.'

24th January, Wednesday

I caught Hilary reading her horoscope, told her what superstitious, unChristian rubbish they are, and what did mine say? It said that the turnout at the midweek service would be poor, even by January's standards, trying to say 'Ephphatha' when your lips are numb with cold is a mistake, and that I must be careful going up steps if I'm wearing anything ankle length. Which shows that even astrologers get lucky sometimes.

25th January, Thursday

School assembly. Told them the story of Dinah and Shechem from Genesis 34. A little girl put her hand up afterwards, and said, 'My name's Dinah!' so proudly I don't think she had been listening. Miss Jolly asked if that was really in the Bible, and I assured her it was.

Intrigued, I checked yesterday's horoscope for myself. What it actually said was 'Be careful who you trust. Someone you love may not be telling you the truth.'

26th January, Friday

Hilary says there is a problem with the car. A funny smell, and she wants me to take it into the garage. Hilary always thinks any smell in the car means it's going to blow up, but it hasn't yet. But I phoned Derek and he says he can fit it in on Wednesday. Always good to have something to look forward to.

27th January, Saturday
Is there no end to the
sales? Hilary came back
from town having saved
even more money. I felt
her credit card. It was
hot.

**28th January, Fourth
Sunday of Epiphany**
No early service in the
vacant benefice this morning, so I could concen-
trate on worship here. The choir were in good voice
in the vestry before and after the service, but not so
good in the choir stalls during it. I preached about
Jesus turning water into wine; and said none of us
can do that, though we can all turn wine into
water. Pause for laugh. Not a sausage. After the
service, Mrs Hopkins pointed out there were only a
couple of spoonfuls left in the coffee jar. But she
still served coffee all round, and nobody noticed
any difference. If I relied on the coffee to keep the
congregation awake, I wouldn't be able to speak
over the snoring.

29th January, Monday
Hilary is right. There is a funny smell in the car. I
opened the bonnet, but the only thing I recognized
under there was the dipstick. And it had taken
me most of *Woman's Hour* to work out how to

open the bonnet. Some things are best left to the experts.

30th January, Tuesday

Trudged about in the slush all day visiting, because the car smells like the proverbial wrestler's jock-strap, monkey's armpit, or Doctor Kelly's breath. I called in at the Temporary Sign for something warming, but the fire was so small it seemed to make the bar colder, if anything. Doris says Arthur the landlord isn't exactly mean, but he knows the names of all his logs.

31st January, Wednesday

Took the car in to Derek, straight after the mid-week service, and left it with him. Called for it at 5 o'clock, and he proudly told me he'd solved the problem. After dismantling the whole engine, checking the heating system, replacing all the hoses and going over the wiring with a fine tooth comb, he found a dead pheasant in the boot, and charged me the price of dinner for two at the Ritz.

February

February

1st February, Thursday

Daffodil out in the churchyard. A little yellow head nodding among the gravestones. I phoned Ray and Dennis and they came with the van, ropes, a large net, and something that looked like a hairdresser's clipper. Ray made blue sparks at the end of it, and informed me gleefully, 'That's *Lectrical*, Vicar!' By the time Daffodil was subdued, the angel had lost its other ear and the point of one wing, and some of the flat grave slabs were actually standing up.

Too late to get to school, so I phoned to apologize. Miss Jolly said they'd manage without me some-how, and then something at her end must have made her laugh, and she had to put the phone down, quite helpless.

2nd February, Friday, Candlemas

Nothing like an alien in your packet of Shreddies to brighten up a cold February morning. Both boys wanted it, but I told them not to be childish, and put it with the others. I only need one more to complete the set.

No jobs worth pursuing in *Church Times* unless I want to be vicar of Ascension Island, which might save on credit card bills. The advert didn't say, but I get the impression that Ascension Island is at least 1,000 miles from the nearest Top Shop.

Candlemas service this evening. Some children inconsolable because they thought it was the one with the orange and the jelly tots. I told them they have 11 months to wait for that, but it would certainly be worth it. But tonight was still a great success, which means nobody actually set anybody else on fire this year, and the damage was fairly limited. Ecclesiastical Insurance must have a good laugh, anyway.

3rd February, Saturday
Spent the morning with the iron and a sheet of brown paper getting the wax out of the chancel carpet before the cleaning ladies came in. It sounds wimpish, but I'd rather face a carpet full of melted wax than the wrath of the cleaning ladies, especially Mrs Hopkins. I still remember when she picketed the church over her demand for a new Hoover, standing by a brazier with a placard, inviting passing motorists to honk if they supported her, and by the time the strike was over, you could actually hear the spiders partying, and then there was more unpleasantness over the danger money. The scorch marks on the wall will have to wait.

4th February, Fourth Sunday before Lent
Drove over to Great Shakes in near darkness for early service. Four people came, which the church-warden said was something of a record, but which way he didn't say. I felt a bit bad because my petrol

money was more than the collection, but the old man made it up out of his own pocket. Here is a parish that appreciates the true cost of its ministry. Back in time for services here. Adrian preached, and as usual, his mother and his sister were planted in the congregation, shouting 'Amen!' and 'Tell it like it is, brother!' And he doesn't say, 'Let's stand and sing hymn number whatever', but 'I'm going to ask you to get up out of your seats'. Who does he think he is?

5th February, Monday

Day off. Tried not answering the phone, but curiosity got the better of me, so tried answering by disguising my voice and saying, 'Cheeving Asylum', but she just carried on anyway. She'd told me her name and her life history before I twigged she was trying to sell me double glazing. I told her I would really love double glazing because the curtains at the vicarage billow out like the sails of the Cutty Sark rounding the Cape of Good Hope, and the boys fly a kite in their bedroom. She said, 'Vicarage? Is that a vicarage?' and hung up.

6th February, Tuesday

Chapter meeting. Everyone trying to sit opposite Shirley was like musical chairs at a children's party. Terry Dickson had put his Filofax on the chair opposite hers, which struck me as a particularly childish thing to do, so I just moved it and sat down. After the business bit, I'd been looking forward to the talk on Metempsychosis but all he seemed to talk about was reincarnation, which I thought meant you came back as a tin of evaporated milk. Much discussion about what we'd all come back as if we had the choice, and nearly everyone said they'd like to try being a woman, if only for the dresses. Shirley said if that's what you want, come back as a priest, but make it a Roman Catholic. How we all laughed.

7th February, Wednesday
Called out to Gruntle's Farm at five in the morning to see a strange phenomenon. Ted Gruntle, who hasn't slept for the best part of a week, told me in his rich rural burr that a two-headed lamb was born in the night. While I was still going 'Wow!' and asking to see it, he told me he'd then noticed it also had two bodies, two tails, and no less than eight legs. The extraordinary creature was also able to divide itself, and be in two places at once. 'It portends, Vicar', he insisted. I agreed with him, as I backed away.

Visitors to the church stayed for the midweek service, then asked me about the ancient frescoes in the chancel. I hated to disappoint them, but I told them they were scorch marks left over from Friday.

8th February, Thursday
At school assembly, I told them the story of Joseph and Potiphar's wife, but they all started to yawn and say they'd seen the musical.

Had a good morning visiting, and called on Mrs Pickles, who thinks I am the last vicar but one, and always calls me Mr Walker, and asks how Millicent is. When I left, she said, 'Let me give you something for the church, Vicar', opened her purse, and gave me a sixpence. An actual sixpence. I thanked her very much, and told her I would buy the church a choc ice.

9th February, Friday
Took holy communion to Mrs Things in the old people's bungalows. I went through the whole service, and when I offered her the wafer, she said, 'This is Friday. I have fish on Friday', and refused it. Mrs Things is so old that when the social worker asked her in a loud voice who the prime minister was, she said, 'That nice Lord Salisbury', and cackled like a maniac.

10th February, Saturday
Little Damian can't go through the churchyard to get to the park because he is the Antichrist and bears the mark of the Beast. So he has to go the long way round, along the wall, avoiding the shadow of the church tower. He tried to give me a Baleful Glare as he went by, but he was sucking a sherbet fountain, which diluted the effect.

11th February, Third Sunday before Lent
Thought the boys' missing snowman had turned up in the churchyard, but it was only a toddler – one of the Potter children, as it turned out – entirely covered in bird droppings, as if a whole flock of starlings had bombed her with uncanny accuracy. By the time the Potters had got her as far as the churchyard tap, she had set completely rigid, and had to be soaked to soften her. My light-hearted suggestion that she would have made such a good statue it was a pity to wash her was not well received.

I preached on the text 'Woe to you when all speak well of you', and tried not to give the impression that all politicians go straight to heaven when they die, and that Gwyneth Paltrow is damned.

To Calling All Saints for evensong. A packed congregation, and neither of them a day under 80.

12th February, Monday
One of those days when it didn't seem to get light, and you think winter is never going to end. I tried reading the boys' *Beano,* but I could hardly see the print. Then Hilary came back from the village, and asked why I was wearing my sunglasses. Quick as a flash, I said it was my day off and I didn't want to

be recognized. And she said she'd know me anywhere because of the dog collar.

13th February, Tuesday
A good morning visiting, and so much coffee, my
hands were shaking by the time I got home, which
is a hazard of the vocation
they don't warn you
about at college. In the
afternoon I set about
tidying the vicar's vestry
(which always sounds
like a 1950s airliner). I
took everything out of the
old chest of drawers, and
replaced the newspaper lining. Now I have a copy
of the *Daily Mirror* with Mr Eden resigning over
Suez, and an empty chest of drawers, because there
was nothing that needed to go back. And what does
one do with a bin bag full of candle stumps? Melt
them down and make a model of Elvis? When I set
about the cobwebs in the corners, spiders actually
wrestled the feather duster from my grip and beat
me about the head with it.

PCC met in the village hall, with everyone present
except Mrs Hooley, who sent her apologies because
she was on the lap-dancing rota at The Laurels Old
Peoples' Home. Lively discussion on whether we
should baptize every baby whose parents request
it, or only those who come to church. Harry Parry

said, 'What we have to ask ourselves is "Can we afford to pass over the fees?"' and I reminded him there are no fees for a baptism. He went pale, and said he would bring it up at Synod, because nobody respects what they don't have to pay for. I managed to persuade them to keep on with the current practice, because it's the church reaching out, and if Jesus was happy to have children around, that's good enough for me, most of the time, when the boys are asleep. While we were discussing the Easter services, Mrs Pryke asked whether we could have it the week after, because her grandchildren were on holiday that week, and she wanted to take them to Legoland.

Read the *Daily Mirror* in bed. Whatever happened to Garth?

14th February, Wednesday

I pointed out to Hilary while we were having breakfast that St Valentine's Day has been hijacked by big business, and now has nothing to do with the celebration of a rather obscure saint about whom we know very little for certain, except that he did for love what the Boston Strangler did for door-to-door salesmen. She banged my coffee down in front of me and said, 'A card wouldn't have killed you!' I wonder what's upset her?

15th February, Thursday

At school assembly, I told them the story of Jael the wife of Heber the Kenite and Sisera, the commander of the Canaanite chariots. I bet they haven't seen that in a musical. Ernie the caretaker came in with a bucket of sawdust, a mop and a bottle of Dettol, and grumbled about having the clearing up to do, and said it was all right for me, I could just go home to my ivory tower. He obviously doesn't know the boys are mine.

16th February, Friday

Ada Things has died, of great but indeterminate age. Even her son can't remember her being anything other than very old, very wrinkled, and eating toffee, slowly and noisily, having lost all her teeth down the back of the sofa.

17th February, Saturday

Saturday is a great day for visiting all those people in the village who are at work during the week. Or for watching old movies on TV. While Sam was playing it for Rick, I wrote a sermon about the Sermon on the Mount, which is a bit like painting a picture of a picture. And every time I read the bit about not worrying about food and drink, it made me wonder what was for supper.

18th February, Second Sunday before Lent

All very well for the Lord to say, 'Do not worry about tomorrow', but he hadn't seen my diary. And going on about the birds of the air being care-free has a bit of a hollow ring to it when you know there's a chicken in the oven.

Evensong comparatively well attended, considering it was cold and drizzly, and that was *inside* the church.

19th February, Monday
Day off. Took myself into town to poke about the bookshops. Went into SPCK to see what people are writing about God these days. Absolute filth on the top shelf. I complained to the woman behind the counter, 'When was this last dusted?'

20th February, Tuesday
Spent the morning at the old people's bungalows, charming the old ladies with my cheeky banter, and trying to get some background information on the late Ada to use at her funeral on Friday. Everyone had a good word for her. It was 'senile'.

It poured with rain all afternoon, so I was in the study writing my piece for the March Magazine, *From Where I Sit,* when a woman knocked at the vicarage door. She said she was trying to find her grandfather, who was in the churchyard. I put my coat on, and said I'd help her look. I asked what he looked like, and she said she didn't know, but his name was Henry Parsons. So I started calling 'Henry!' and I thought she said, 'He won't hear you, he's deaf', so I started calling louder. Didn't I feel a fool when she told me her grandfather had died in 1956. All that paddling about in the wet for nothing.

The Bible study group looked at Joel. I pointed
out that chapter 2 is where the song 'Fear not, re-
joice and be glad' comes from. Sixteen blank looks.
So I sang the first verse to them. Sixteen pained
looks. 'Maybe we should sing it in church some
time', I suggested, and there was a lot of uncomfortable shifting in chairs. This is a congregation
that has a problem with the *and Modern* bit of
Hymns Ancient and Modern.

21st February, Wednesday
I knew it would happen one day. The boys came
home from school and asked, 'Where do we come
from?' So I sat them
down and told them
about what happens
when two people are in
love, and how special it is,
and how they grew inside Hilary,
and she went to the hospital and they were born.
They thought about it, then they said, 'Oh, Simon
comes from Reading.'

In the evening, I got my old guitar out and tuned
it. I asked Hilary what she thought of me playing
it at family service one Sunday, and getting the
congregation singing some new songs. She said it
would be very unwise, as the congregation here
aren't ready for innovative worship songs like
'Kumbaya' and 'Go tell it on the mountain'. They
still think anything written after Psalm 150 is

modern, and dangerous with it. Sadly, I agreed with her, and put it away.

22nd February, Thursday
School assembly. Told the children the story of David and Bathsheba. A little boy put his hand up afterwards and asked what a Hittite was.

23rd February, Friday
Funeral of Ada Things delayed half an hour. Henry Dolt and the men arrived with the coffin shoulder high, and Henry asked whether the family had already gone into church. I said I thought he was bringing them in the limousine. He said 'Ah', turned the bearers around, and went off to fetch the family. Did it never occur to him that the hearse was being followed by an empty car?

24th February, Saturday
Phone call from Michael Speed, asking if he could be baptized. I said he was on the Electoral Roll, so he must have been baptized already, and he said yes, but he was changing his name, so he wanted to be baptized again. I told him this wasn't necessary, or as far as I knew, legal. And everyone knows him as Micky Speed, the Demon Driver of Cheeving Halfpenny. You can hear him coming a long way off, and a long time after he's gone. 'But what are you changing your name to?' I asked. 'P582XAA', he said. I asked him why, as you would. He said,

'I've always wanted one of them personalized number plates.'

25th February, Sunday before Lent
Over to Huffleigh for early service. This interregnum drags on, because nobody will take on a group of parishes the size of the Gobi Desert. But the petrol money comes in handy, if only for buying petrol.

I was late getting back, and Adrian had the presence of mind to start the service without me. But then when I emerged from the vestry, he said, 'And now let's give a real warm welcome to . . . the vicar!'

26th February, Monday
The trouble with a day off when you're the vicar is that if somebody comes up to you in the queue at the butcher's and asks, 'What must I do to inherit eternal life?', you can't just ignore it. Not that it ever happens, mind you, but it could.

27th February, Shrove Tuesday
Hilary shouted, 'What pancake party?' when I asked why she hadn't done anything yet except watch *Countdown*. I said the one that was in the magazine and the Sunday notice sheet and she asked me when I

thought she had time to read the magazine or the Sunday notice sheet, and I pointed out that she was actually writing down her letters and numbers on the back of one. Anyway, she would have refused altogether to cook a single pancake if I hadn't threatened her credit card with the kitchen scissors and offered to help, which I did by going down to the General Stores and buying more flour, eggs, milk and lemons. Just about everyone I passed said, 'See you later then, Vicar', which was nice.

By the time I got back, Hilary had already produced a stack of pancakes that looked almost architectural, the smoke alarm was pinging like a dustcart in reverse and Hilary's hair was clinging to her forehead like Katharine Hepburn in *The African Queen*. I loved it when the boys came in and asked, 'Mummy, what's for tea?' Some of the choir had to be rationed to two pancakes each, or some of the adults would have gone without, but I thought the evening was a great success. Old Mr Teague asked Hilary, 'Did you toss all these?' and she said, 'No, I left that to Ron – he's a great tosser', which just shows how modest she is, doing all the work and giving me all the credit. When the last people had gone, I went into the kitchen to thank Hilary, and out of the smoke, a large knife embedded itself into the wall beside my head. I must call the arch-deacon, and have the kitchen exorcised.

I have decided to give up alcohol for Lent, and I was just putting a bottle of whisky out of the way of temptation, when an angel appeared unto me and spake saying, 'Wend thy maze.' I couldn't for the life of me work out what it meant, but before I could ask, it had gone. Thinking about it, I guess it means life will always be complicated, but I'll just have to find my way through. I'll drink to that, but not until Easter.

28th February, Ash Wednesday
Found Mr Teague in the kitchen, left over from last night. Gave him a cup of tea and an aspirin, and sent him on his way. Evening service with imposition of ashes, made by burning last year's palm crosses. The trouble with our fire extinguishers is that they empty themselves entirely once they're set off. And by the time I'd worked out what 'Stand upside down and strike knob on floor' actually meant (or at least what it doesn't mean), Adrian had doused it with the water from the cruet, anyway.

March

1st March, Thursday, St David
Told the children the story of Amnon and Tamar at assembly. Miss Jolly seemed a little agitated afterwards, and asked whether we might tackle some New Testament subjects.

I said I'd give it some thought, but there is plenty about the Great Whore in Revelation which ought to hold their attention.

I found Evan wandering about behind the General Stores. 'You can't see a leek, can you, Vicar?' he asked. I said 'Why, have you lost one?' and he said, 'I asked Mrs General if I could have a leek, and she said, "Yes, go out the back", but I'm blowed if I can find one.'

2nd March, Friday
No jobs worth pursuing in *Church Times* unless I want to be vicar of somewhere in Wales that sounds like bronchitis. I love the way these adverts say they're looking for a man or woman of exceptional ability, which means we're all too modest to apply. Hilary reminded me of the holiday we once had in Wales when they only had a service in English once a month and it wasn't the Sunday we were there. And the boys were only babies, and we found that the Welsh could understand 'Waah!' in English, and we could understand 'Shhh!' in Welsh. But as it was a pentecostal church, we put it down to that.

3rd March, Saturday

The first Saturday it's felt like spring, so I went out to the sportsfield to watch Cheeving Halfpenny play Peedle Magna. As  I've married half the team, or baptized their children, I feel it's a good idea to give them my support. Nigel the captain came up to me at half-time and said I was having a bad effect on the lads because my dog collar was putting them off abusing the opposition in the traditional fashion, which was why they were 3–0 down. So I left them to it, and found out later they won 6–3, a triumph of bad language over skill.

Back home to the news that old Joseph Clutch has died, so I changed my scarf and went down to see his daughter. The old man had lived in the village for nearly 90 years, and had never been further than Blicester, nor wanted to. During the war he claimed village idiot was a reserved occupation, and it worked.

4th March, First Sunday of Lent

Preached about temptation at the morning service, and afterwards, I'd arranged for one chocolate Digestive among the Rich Teas to see if anything I'd said had sunk in. Not a chance.

In the ensuing battle, the only winner was temptation, and the chocolate Digestive was reduced to its component molecules.

After lunch (not the same without a beer), the annual Blessing of Badgers, which has now somehow extended to include all mammals of the order *Mustelidae*, so I also found myself blessing the stoats, weasels and, not that I could see any around, polecats, which seemed a bit silly, really, and detracts from the solemnity of the occasion.

5th March, Monday

Hilary out at her kick-boxing class all morning. Henry Dolt called to make arrangements for Joseph Clutch's funeral, which I had to remind him is on Friday. 'This Friday?' he said, in some alarm. While he was correcting his diary, I asked him how he came to be a funeral director, and he said it sort of grew out of his building business. I asked him what he built. 'The two new houses on the road to Blicester,' he said. 'You know the ones, with the big props holding the fronts up. And the house between the end of the lane and Ferret's Bottom. Oh no,' he added, 'That fell down before you came here.' Why does that not surprise me?

6th March, Tuesday
Chapter meeting. Talk on Giving up Lent. The vote
was nine in favour, one against and one abstention,
because Canon Hubble said he'd given up voting
until Easter. Managed to sit opposite Shirley, and
apologized profusely to Richard Head for elbowing him. I think I managed to convince him it was
an accident. I observed that Keith has no interest in
Shirley's knees at all, and that he's the most high
churchman among us. Is there any connection, I
ask myself?

7th March, Wednesday
Nearly late for the midweek service. Jason Orrell's
rottweiller, Lennox, had just produced a heap the
size of an Austin Metro, right outside the doctor's
surgery, where I'd been to collect my ointment.
When I remonstrated, Orrell said, 'You can't keep
on taking out, Vicar. You got to put something
back. That's ecology, that is.' Then he emptied his
beer can, squashed it in one hand, put it on top of
the heap, and said, 'And that's art!' It was 9.30 in
the morning. Lennox, for his part, coughed up a
small strap with a bell on it, and Jason went off,
complaining about thoughtless people who put
collars on their cats. 'Could've choked him', he said.

8th March, Thursday
Miss Jolly told me the school is reviewing its policy
on assembly, and they won't be needing me after
this half-term. Which is sad, because I feel the

children were really beginning to get the benefit. Only this morning, a little boy in the playground told another to 'Know off!'

Called on Mrs Hole, who showed me delightedly how much better her arthritis was, and got stuck like it. Phoned Dr Kelly, who said he'd be there as soon as possible, so I left rather than face his breath, and as a precaution, put Mrs Hole's canary in the other room.

9th March, Friday
Funeral in the afternoon of Joseph Clutch, the last official village idiot of Cheeving Halfpenny, who used to carry an umbrella without any fabric on it when it wasn't raining. I thought Henry Dolt did a faultless job, right up to when he took the wreath off the coffin at the graveside, and the brass plate said Josephine Clutch in letters an inch high. Good to see that Henry hasn't lost his touch. Mrs Brake, Joseph's daughter, looked at the plate and said, 'It's what he would have wanted.'

10th March, Saturday
Annual spring clean. This used to be a mere ritual, but the state of the church now has made it a necessity. The lengthening days mean that the dirt shows, and last week, Mrs Pryke spent several minutes trying to hoover up a small patch of sunlight in the aisle, and by the time she realized her mistake, the stone was considerably eroded. All cleaning ladies

arrived at 10 o'clock sharp, heavily armed and wearing their oldest clothes, as instructed, which means Mrs Hopkins was wearing a bustle. Some of the creatures lurking in the church are unknown to science (though not to theology), but Mrs Hopkins made a speech to the ladies like Henry V at Agincourt, and then it looked like the Elgin Marbles as pitched battles were fought, broom against fang, dust flew, cobwebs ripped, and I crept off to make tea. When I came back, it was all over. Mrs Hopkins spat out her gumshield, accepted a mug of tea, and pointed to the Hoover, which was jumping about, apparently of its own volition. 'I'll take that to the woods and give them their freedom', she said. 'Why don't you just kill them?' I asked. 'You can't kill them,' she said. 'They're undead already.'

11th March, Second Sunday of Lent

Over to Duffleigh for the early service. Church locked. Apparently I should have gone to Puffleigh, where apparently there was a huge congregation banging its spoons, so to speak, and chanting 'Why are we waiting?' to a seasonal melody. An easy enough mistake to make.

Back here, I preached on John 3.16, although I always think I needn't bother. Just read the text. But when I tried it once, there was old Mr Blewitt banging on the vestry door after the service demanding his money back.

12th March, Monday

Thwarted in my plan to spend my day off putting my collection of wafers in alphabetical order, because Hilary reminded me that Wednesday is the boys' birthday, and made me drive her to town. Not entirely a wasted trip, though. Just because I insisted on trying out toys before buying them, Hilary says she's never coming shopping with me again. I asked her to put it in writing. But then she dragged me around shops where she tried on clothes before buying them, without apparently seeing the irony. And it doesn't feel like a proper day off if I keep bumping into parishioners.

13th March, Tuesday

Hilary managed to make a cake shaped like a Super Star Destroyer, and iced it beautifully, except she put the shield generators in front of the turbo-laser pods. But she persuaded me not to mention it to the boys, or my valuable collection of late twentieth-century peoples' wafers might depreciate considerably.

Mrs O'Chairs phoned in the evening and asked me to change the altar frontal on Saturday from

Lenten purple to green for St Patrick. I said there wasn't a service on Saturday, so nobody would see it, but she said she'd make a point of going in specially to look.

14th March, Wednesday
The boys' birthday. Whoever gave them a chemistry set ought to be shot. Or at least be made to clean up the mess. A dozen of their little friends came to tea, and it was not a pretty sight. In the evening, Hilary and I were reminiscing about when they were born, and when they were toddlers, and all the little milestones in their lives, like their first  faltering steps, their first words, their first day at school, and their first attempt to put a rabbit into space, when there was a noise from upstairs like a small explosion. Up we rushed, and found smoke coming out from under their door. They were more frightened than hurt, and a quick coat of emulsion will cover the marks on the wall. 'What were you trying to do?' asked Hilary. 'Create life', they said.

15th March, Thursday
I spotted Miss Threadgold tottering along on her high heels, and ducked into the General Stores

before she saw me, and pretended to be looking at sweets. Cheeving Halfpenny is even more of a backwater than I thought, because Mrs General still sells Opal Fruits and Marathons. I bet she's got some Spangles tucked away somewhere. But Miss Threadgold had spotted me, caught me by the cake decorations and said, 'You haven't been to see me for a long time, Vicar.' I was about to explain that I'd been sober, when she said, 'Come tomorrow evening. It will be good for my soul.' I said I'd come if she promised not to wear the black stockings or anything, and she promised.

16th March, Friday

Miss Threadgold's door opened by itself to my tentative knock, and she called, 'Come in, Vicar.' She was in the sitting room, and true to her promise, she wasn't wearing the black stockings, or anything, if you get my drift. I made my excuses and left, thinking a drink or two would blot out the terrible spectacle imprinted on my brain, and made my way to the Temporary Sign. I remembered just in time I've given it up for Lent, and ordered orange juice.

Jason Orrell had too much to drink, which is par for the course, and made a pass at Doris the barmaid, which

isn't. She was over the bar like an Olympic hurdler, seized him in a half-nelson, marched him across the floor with his toes off the ground, and threw him bodily into the street. A moment later, his head appeared back round the door. 'Respect!' he said, and disappeared into the night.

17th March, Saturday, St Patrick

On the grounds that it would make Mrs O'Chairs happy, I changed the altar frontal to green, which is a job I hate. It's like reefing the sails on HMS Bounty, and an excellent way of breaking your fingernails. Then just before I locked up in the evening, I changed it back for the purple one, thinking Fletcher Christian probably had the right idea.

Football team at home again, so I turned out on the touchline, wearing my scarf to cover the dog collar. Half-time, and two goals down, and Nigel came over. 'It's no good Vicar,' he said, 'They still know it's you.'

18th March, Third Sunday of Lent

I preached on the text 'Let it alone for one more year, until I dig round it and put manure on it'. Old Len said afterwards, 'That were an all right sermon, Vicar, with the dung.' I said I preferred the word 'manure'. Mrs Len said that if I heard what he usually called it, I'd settle for dung. I asked Mrs O'Chairs if she'd looked in at the church yesterday, and she said no, her husband had taken her to see her old mother, and they'd had a grand day, thanks.

19th March, Monday
A little card from the Dean of Blicester saying they're praying for our parish at evensong in the cathedral on 25 April, and did I want to be there, and do I want to robe up. Who can resist dressing up and processing in the cathedral? Not me.

20th March, Tuesday
Came home from visiting to find Hilary gazing up in awe at a pile of manure the size of Mont Blanc on the drive, blotting out the sun, and preventing her getting the car out. She said she had no idea where it came from, so I explained about the back ends of cows. Then she said I had to move it or she wouldn't be able to take the boys swimming, and I said if I didn't move it she could take them climbing, and we had a lively discussion about where I might move it to. It took me an hour and a half just to shovel it to one side so Hilary could get the car down the drive. I was glad to stop when the phone rang. It was Old Len asking had I found it, and on a scale of one to ten,

how pleased was I with it? Apparently, he'd got the impression from Sunday's sermon that I was passionate about the stuff, and there was nothing like a pile of dung on the drive for keeping the flies out of the kitchen.

21st March, Wednesday
The pile of manure in front of the vicarage now has a cap of snow like Mount Fuji. Very artistic, but mysterious, too, as it hasn't actually snowed since January. On closer examination it proved to be bird droppings, as if a whole flock of starlings had chosen to use it all at once. Isn't nature wonderful?

22nd March, Thursday
Just as I was writing my piece, *From Where I Sit*, for the parish magazine for April, I had a brainwave. A free bag of manure with every copy. Who says I can't do joined-up thinking?

23rd March, Friday
Called in at the Temporary Sign at lunchtime, on the grounds that the vicar ought to be where his people are, only this time they weren't. Just P582XAA having a pint and a ploughman's lunch, and a ploughman looking pretty miffed about it. Doris the barmaid says Jason has been treating her with great courtesy, and has brought her flowers. 'How can I stop him?' she asked. I said she shouldn't try, and she said, 'You don't understand.'

Later, near Ferret's Bottom, I saw Jason with

Lennox, out foraging for Jack Russells to supple-
ment his diet of tinned meat and biscuits. Goodness
only knows what the dog eats. I couldn't resist
asking him about Doris. 'Doris!' he said, and his
rugged features took on a softer cast for a moment.
Imagine Mount Rushmore melting, and you get the
general idea. Lennox made choking noises and spat
out a small medallion, and Jason said he had to go.
'Got flowers to nick', he explained.

24th March, Saturday
Mrs Macreedy, Mrs Smallie and Mrs Todger were
picking flowers in the vicarage garden all morning
to make posies for tomorrow. I reminded the boys
that it was Mothering Sunday, and slipped them
some money to buy Hilary some flowers.

25th March, Mothering Sunday
The boys gave Hilary some lovely flowers, but
they'd left the card in, which said, 'We can never
tell you Grandad, How much we wanted you to
stay, But God must have needed an Angel, so he
took you away. Love from Shirl.' The worst of it
is, the standard of doggerel in the churchyard is
actually improving. As they go, that was quite
good.

As we arrived at church, all those who had put
their clocks back an hour instead of forward were
milling about confused, but once we'd assured
them the church clock was right, and April Fools'

Day is next week, they came in and joined us. The service was a great success, with all the children coming up to collect little posies to give to their mothers, and some of the grown ups coming to get flowers for theirs, and Mrs Hope, who is 85, hobbling up to get some for her mother, who is 103.

As we came out, all those who had forgotten to put their clocks forward were coming in, and I hated to send them away disappointed, but it was that, or miss lunch.

26th March, Monday, The Annunciation

I saw Mrs O'Chairs in the post office, and said, 'Top of the morning to you, Mrs O'Chairs', to show I don't bear her a grudge, and she said, 'Sure and call me Patty.'

27th March, Tuesday

Sally Things, Ada's great-granddaughter, is marrying Martin O'Malley, the tennis club secretary, and she isn't even pregnant. Who says Cheeving Halfpenny doesn't have class?

Bible study group looked at Amos. We all thought a basket of fruit was a bit boring for a vision. More like a raffle prize than a divine revelation. But I had a commentary hidden under the table, so I could explain that in Hebrew 'fruit' rhymes with 'end', so it's a vision of the end, and pretend I'd known that all along, which is what we vicars do. And if we can use words like 'eschatology' as well, so much the better.

28th March, Wednesday
The Colonel told me after the midweek service that Mrs Hooley is in hospital. He said 'I expect you already know', as if God leaves messages on my answerphone. I just realized that Sally Things will be Sally O'Malley, which is funny, but only a bit.

29th March, Thursday
Off to the district hospital to visit Mrs Hooley. At the reception desk, they told me she was in Pol Pot Ward. So off I set with map, compass and stout boots. The sister on Pol Pot told me she'd been transferred to Josef Stalin Ward, which is about three-quarters of a mile away, the other side of the building, next to the Idi Amin Serious Sprains Unit. I could have gone outside, and taken the bus to the other entrance, but I decided to walk instead, pausing only to brew tea on my primus stove and eat some Kendal Mint Cake. At Josef Stalin, they told me Mrs Hooley had been sent home. So I walked the other three-quarters of a mile back to the car, and drove back.

30th March, Friday
Called on Mrs Hooley. She hobbled to the door, gave me a reproachful look, wagged her finger at me, and said 'I've been in hospital, Vicar, and you never came to see me.'

31st March, Saturday

I gave up on anyone from the diocese ever coming to change the washer on the kitchen tap, despite me asking every month for the last year and a half, so I decided to do it myself. Mrs General charged me 5p for the washer, I found a wrench in the garage, and then I couldn't reach under the sink to turn the water off. So I moved the fridge out, and pulled the whole socket out of the wall. I made a mental note to fix it later, and managed to change the tap washer, which is a piece of cake really. I don't know why Church House couldn't have had it done. Then as I turned the water back on, I hit my head on the underneath of the sink, and you know how scalps bleed, so Hilary insisted on sticking me in the car, with the boys in the back, and driving me to the hospital. Three hours and two stitches later, Mrs General sold me a new socket to replace the broken one, and despite the boys' protests because I had to turn the electricity off for ten minutes, did a pretty good job, if I say so myself. Then Hilary pointed out two small details – the new tap washer, and the kitchen tap still dripping. I told her I had a headache.

April

1st April, Fifth Sunday of Lent

Supposed to go to Griping St Todger to fill in at early service, but surmised that there is probably no such place as Griping St Todger, and the whole thing was an elaborate ruse I was too clever to fall for.

Here, I preached last year's Harvest Festival sermon, complete with references to how nice the church looked, full of vegetables. I think nobody appreciated the joke because nobody noticed the difference.

Henry Stebbings, who delivers the church magazines at the top end of the village asked me what he was supposed to do with 30 bags of manure, and if I thought he was going to lug them around with the magazines then I could think again.

2nd April, Monday

Bluebell out in churchyard. Called Ray and Dennis, who agreed it was early, but in a sheltered spot, so not really surprising.

Churchwarden of Griping St Todger phoned to say they missed me yesterday and asked if I was ill. Whoops.

3rd April, Tuesday

Annual parochial meeting. Spent most of the day writing my little report where I look back on the last year, and say thank you to everybody, from Adrian the Reader, Dennis Elbeau the organist, right down to the ladies who clean the church and make the coffee and the people who are supposed to keep the churchyard under control, but don't. Everybody voted for everybody else as usual, and Colonel Toop and Mrs Thomas are churchwardens again for the foreseeable future. Harry Parry the treasurer tried to keep cheerful, saying there's sometimes nearly enough in the collection these days to pay for the Rich Tea biscuits. I singled him out for special thanks because being church treasurer must be a bit like being an Avon rep in Alcatraz.

4th April, Wednesday
Called on the Brigadier after the midweek service, in that brief window between his getting up and getting drunk. He asked me if that jumped-up little Colonel was still churchwarden, and I said yes, and reminded him that strictly speaking, the Colonel and he, the Brigadier, were both civilians. He turned his good eye on me fiercely and said, '*Never* use that word to me! When I was in Africa . . .' as a prelude to a long and rambling story about chickens, natives, and a gun he'd once had that could blow a hole you could see through in an elephant. The natives, he said, called it *ngana-m'wango-kozi-m'-bunabuna-m'wazi-kabongo*, which means, in their language, 'gun'.

5th April, Thursday
Sharon who runs the playschool says Jason Orrell is the father of her forthcoming baby. As he is

already the acknowledged father of half the play-school, and the unacknowledged father of the rest, nobody is at all surprised. Jason spreads his genetic material around the village like Jehovah's Witnesses the *Watchtower,* and claims to be doing what he can to save the primary school, so we should thank him. Personally, I think he's trying to breed lots of Orrells, so that one day, they will outnumber the Bloats.

6th April, Friday
No jobs worth pursuing in *Church Times* unless I want to be chaplain to a psychiatric hospital. But I need a change, not more of the same. When you get ordained, the bishop gives you a Bible, and a licence with his seal on it. God gives you the Holy Spirit and a bunch of nutters.

7th April, Saturday
Caught a bunch of wild flowers by the porch, trying to sneak into church during Lent. But we have to be strict about that sort of thing. Where would it end?

The boys were invited to little Justin Stebbings' birthday party, so Hilary took them to Blicester to buy presents. I advised them to get him something they would like themselves, and they would both have come back with Big Macs if Hilary hadn't suggested Lego instead. Off they went in the afternoon, and when Hilary fetched them, tired but happy, they had a big bag of party loot, and a bag of manure each.

8th April, Palm Sunday

All is explained. There is a roc's nest in the tower, unseen behind the parapet.

Little Nicholas Stebbings was carried off by the male to feed the chicks. A bird with a 15-foot wingspan carrying a fully robed treble is an awesome spectacle, and another instance of the wonders of creation turning one's thoughts to the creator. The choirmaster assures me Nicholas would never have made a soloist anyway, but the really bad news is we won't be able to fly the flag next Sunday, for fear of disturbing the nest.

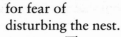

The procession entered the church a little too fast, I thought, losing some dignity, but the distribution of palms passed off with only minor scuffles. Note for next year; the donkey was a mistake.

9th April, Monday

Hilary was at her glass-blowing class at Blicester College all morning, so I took myself off for a walk, the only way I can get away from the demands of my parishioners. The woods in spring are particularly beautiful, and I found myself humming 'How great thou art' despite it being a Monday. My circuit brought me back through Ferrets' Bottom, where the sounds of daytime TV drifted from the open windows. There was Shane Bloat, in his usual string vest, tinkering under the bonnet of his car. I stopped to pass the time of day, and along came Jason with a jack, and started to take off one of the wheels. Shane told him to go away in no uncertain terms, and Jason said, 'Fair do's! If you can have the battery, I'm having the wheels!' So the feud between the Bloats and the Orrells, which has been going on since the days of steam, took another turn for the worse. Shane with his spanner, versus Jason with his wheelbrace. Despite my pleas to turn the other cheek, love thy neighbour, and not marry with the daughters of the Gergashites, they banged away at each other until Shane's wife called him in for his lunch.

10th April, Tuesday

Chapter meeting. Talk on Hypostasis. The only thing I understood all morning was Molly the rural dean's wife asking if I took sugar. Shirley had said she would be late, and it was quite amusing to see everyone jockeying to sit opposite the empty chair. Terry finally achieved it, after a little unseemly pushing and shoving, and the expression on his face when she came in wearing trousers was a real picture. Serves him right for being a dirty old man.

11th April, Wednesday
Invitation to the induction and installation of the new rector at the Peedles. Clergy to robe and process, bunfight afterwards in village hall. No more turning out to early services with no congregations, but no more petrol money either, which has kept the wolf from the door for a while now. I Ar-es-vee-peed right away, and put a ring around it on the calendar. It's on a Thursday, so I shall start fasting on the Tuesday to do it justice.

12th April, Maundy Thursday
We always have our evening holy communion service in somebody's house, and this year Miss Tredgett offered her hospitality. Miss Tredgett has more cats than chairs. She insisted on giving us all tea and cake first, so the commemoration of the last supper grew out of a fellowship meal. We were all squashed into her little living room, and it gave the service a real sense of intimacy, passing the plate and the cup around. 'What a pity,' Miss Tredgett said, 'We can't do this more often.' And I reminded her that with the quinquennial inspection on the church coming up, we might have to.

April

13th April, Good Friday

I didn't expect anyone to come for the whole three hours' service, so I wasn't disappointed. But I had expected some of the choir to be there some of the time. Next year I shall tell them they can only have an Easter egg on Sunday if they have a voucher which I shall give out on Friday. If nothing else, it should reduce the bill for Easter eggs.

14th April, Easter Eve

It is a little-known fact that oasis is actually a virulent green fungus that grows in dark cupboards in churches, mostly during Lent. Flower ladies put in small bits on Shrove Tuesday, and six weeks later, huge quantities of the stuff spew out like an avalanche as soon as the cupboard door is touched. Mrs Macreedy was more frightened than hurt, and said she was going to wash her hair anyway, and most of it we shovelled up and took outside in wheelbarrows, despite Mrs Smallie insisting it's bad luck to throw it out. She says her mother once threw out some oasis, and within the year, her father ran off with the meals-on-wheels lady. The church looks lovely, anyway, with flowers and greenery sprouting out of every orifice. Even the woodworm holes in the pulpit have been filled with primroses, a very charming effect. I broke up a number of small tiffs over who decorated which window sill before they developed into actual fistfights, except the one between Mrs Todger and

Miss Pryke, who insisted that she inherited the north aisle window sill from her late mother. Mrs Todger claimed that the right died with old Mrs Pryke, and had Tai Kwon Do to back her up. Miss Pryke has a black belt at Ikebana, but it was no contest. Then nobody was willing to take Miss Pryke to A and E in case somebody else did their window while they were gone.

Leftover oasis is back in the cupboard, against my better judgment. The next person it engulfs might be less forgiving than Mrs Macreedy.

15th April, Easter Sunday
Anybody who can't preach a blinder on Easter Sunday really shouldn't be preaching at all. Full turn out, the choir in their robes which only get washed once a year and this is it, and everyone joined in the Alleluias.

Both boys overdosed on chocolate eggs, which is par for the course, but then they found if they put one on their heads they could look like Klingons, which isn't.

16th April, Easter Monday
Just as I was making up for six weeks of abstinence, an angel appeared unto me and spake, saying, 'Be a betting person.' I shall start tomorrow.

I'm supposed to have this week off, to make up for the rigours of holy week, but twitchers have found out about the roc's nest, and have been infesting the churchyard, all armed with huge

green telescopes, which have
their own little anoraks as
well. So far, only the odd
bobble hat has been
snatched off by the mighty
bird's talons, although
there was a near thing
when one hapless twitcher
was seized, and only his
friends holding on to his
ankles prevented him getting

acquainted with the youngsters. 'That was the
male', he said. I asked him how he could tell, and he
said, 'The female's bigger.'

Great excitement when one of the twitchers
discovered that the corbels under the eaves of the
nave represent the sins of the flesh, and they were
diverted for a few minutes while they tried to estab-
lish exactly what the sins of the flesh are. They are
admittedly badly weathered, but most of them seem
to involve bottoms.

17th April, Tuesday

While I was in town, I put a tenner to win on Angel
Delight running in the 3.30 at Uttoxeter. It seemed
like a good omen, but the wretched animal was
unplaced. There are probably theological implications to this, but I'm blowed if I can see what they
are. The next time I see an angel I shall ask it to put
it in writing.

18th April, Wednesday

The first cuckoo of spring! He arrived on the doorstep saying he wanted to make his confession.

I got Hilary to make him a cup of tea while I panicked. I managed to fix up a confessional out of the box the computer came in and one of the shelves from the oven, and led him into church. He confessed [*passage deleted for obvious reasons*] and although I didn't believe a word of it, I told him as a penance to clear the roc-poo out of the church gutters. He said, 'I thought you'd make me say some Hail Marys' and I said he could if he liked while he was cleaning out the gutters.

19th April, Thursday

Down at the Temporary Sign, P582XAA, who is one of Jason's friends, was teasing him about his obvious infatuation with Doris the barmaid. 'Isn't she a bit old for you?' he asked. Jason gave a horrible leer, and said 'Remember what Benjamin Franklin said!' 'Ah yes!' I put in, 'Older women are more grateful.' 'No,' said Jason, 'Some are weather-wise, some are otherwise.'

20th April, Friday

Anxious phone call from Mrs Keats, who lives opposite the church, saying that the gargoyles are

on the move again. The last
time this happened, she
reminded me, we had to rewrite
the church history on those
table tennis bats that hang on
the back pews. I went out to

check, but it was only the young rocs peeping over
the parapet of the tower. An easy mistake to make,
although the gargoyles have teeth, as many a pigeon
has found to its cost.

21st April, Saturday
I persuaded Mrs Smallie to help me clear out the
oasis, by giving her a stern lecture about superstition. Her mother apparently made them up to stop
people doing anything she disapproved of, like
bringing shoes into the house, taking dogs on buses
or having sex. I assured her that superstition had
no place in a Christian life, and that I'm not superstitious about anything, and nothing terrible has
happened to me yet, touch wood.

22nd April, Second Sunday of Easter
Preached on Jesus' appearance to Thomas. Gave it
my best, but personally, I'm on Thomas' side. Like
the time Geoff Brown was in the Temporary Sign,
and allegedly bought someone else a drink. I heard
about it, but I didn't believe it, and tried to track
down the mystery recipient, but without success.
And if Geoff Brown had really bought anyone else

a drink, they wouldn't have drunk it, they'd have had it stuffed and mounted. Some things you don't believe unless you see them. So when Mrs Macreedy asked me over coffee, 'Do you really believe Jesus rose from the dead?' I said, 'I hope so, because I was talking to him this morning.'

23rd April, Monday, St George
Couldn't fly the flag from the church tower, unless I wanted to be ripped limb from limb and fed to the chicks. So I wore a rose in my buttonhole all day. Whenever anybody tells me their ancestors came over with William the Conqueror, I tell them my ancestors were on the beach with Harold, trying to stop their ancestors coming over. The Colonel was in the Temporary Sign, saw my buttonhole and said, 'Bravo! There'll always be an England, what?' Then he asked me if I'd care to join him in a Scotch.

24th April, Tuesday
Nothing like finding a Warrior Robot in your Frosties to put you in a good mood for the day. Both the boys claimed it, so to stop them quarrelling I put it with the rest of my collection.

Bible study in the evening got a bit bogged down over the problem of Deutero-Obadiah, the unknown follower of the master who, according to German scholars like Hans Klapping and Karl Sperglager, must have completed the mighty opus. After I'd outlined the arguments for and against,

Mrs Hope looked thoughtful, and said, 'Edom. Is that where the cheese comes from?'

25th April, Wednesday
To Blicester Cathedral for evensong, which is at 3 o'clock, which always strikes me as a bit early, even in April. Blicester Cathedral is of course unique, because it is average. Of all English cathedrals, the nave is average length, the tower is average height, and it has the average number of windows. No other cathedral, however, has stained-glass windows depicting characters from *Watch with Mother*. The choir, it has to be said, is average, although for sheer evil, I'd back our parish church choir against the whole lot of them.

Vergers with little staves with knobs on led us into the stalls, and nobody tripped over anything, which is just as well because Japanese tourists were videoing everything. The choir sang like angels in between being little monsters, playing three card brag, and bullying the little ones with glasses. When it came to the prayers, the Dean managed to get the name of our parish wrong, the name of the church wrong, and my name wrong. Fortunately, God is omniscient.

26th April, Thursday
Mrs Smallie came round very distressed because her husband has run off with the captain of the ladies' darts team from the Temporary Sign. She

The Secret Diary of St Gargoyles

blames herself for letting me throw out the oasis, and actually colluding with me by pushing the wheelbarrow. I told her this was superstitious nonsense, and a far more likely explanation is that the captain of the ladies' darts team shares her husband's interest in darts and looks like Jennifer Aniston, and that Mrs Smallie believed what her mother told her about sex bringing bad luck.

27th April, Friday
Goodness knows why the cartoon in *Church Times* was supposed to be funny. There is no such vestment as a risible. Spent the day visiting, always a rewarding ministry, but more so today. Just as I was about to leave, Mrs Grollie said, 'Oh, but Vicar! I haven't offered you anything. Would you like a statue of Moses?' Fortunately, it's only a little one. I shall put it with the rest.

28th April, Saturday
The rocs have fledged and left the nest. RAF Chigfield picked them up on radar and scrambled a squadron of Tornados, and according to the local news they were last seen heading towards Arabia. Goodness knows what might happen if they get picked up on radar there. I can't say I'm sorry to see them go. They may have been rare and handsome, but they thought vestments were dietary fibre.

70

29th April, Third Sunday of Easter

I'd promised Adrian the Reader he could preach at least once over Easter, and today was the day. In the vestry before the service, he was preparing himself by blowing out his breath and shadow boxing. Personally, I rely on a few moments of quiet prayer. This time, his mother and his sister were primed to shout 'Alleluia!' at short intervals, and did so, but I couldn't fault him on content, and his style at least burns up the calories.

30th April, Monday

When I stand for parliament I shall represent the 'Baby on Board' party. It doesn't mean anything, but it seems a pity to waste all those car stickers. Tim Goody passed me in the High Street, and the baby must have arrived, because there was the sticker in his rear window. Then by the General Stores there was Sharon's car with an 'Expectant Mother on Board' sticker. What next? Cars bouncing about in the lay-bys with 'Trying for a Baby' stickers? And what are we supposed to do? Not drive into the back of a car because there's a baby in it? Drive quietly so we don't wake it up? Anyway, I shall go and visit the Goodys and see the new arrival as soon as possible.

May

May

1st May, Tuesday
While I was out doing some visiting, Pop called down to me from the cab of his blue lorry. I agreed with him that everything was just perfick. 'Vicar,' he said. 'Will you marry Greengage, my second eldest?' I told him I was already married. He said, 'Just a fort. Would have been perfick', and drove off.

2nd May, Wednesday
I called to see Mrs Goody and her new baby, who looks as much like a potato as it's possible for a baby to look, but I pretended to admire him anyway, until Mrs Goody told me it was a girl.
She has two children already, so she's probably right, and she said very firmly that this is the last. 'I don't want a Chinese one', she said. I must have let my puzzlement show, because she said, 'I read it in the paper – every fourth baby that's born is Chinese.'

3rd May, Thursday, St Histamine
The church bright with yellow rape flowers for St Histamine's Day. Histamine was a virtuous Roman maiden who vowed never to cut her hair, so it grew into a braid six feet long that cracked like a whip every time she sneezed, which she did quite often, as she suffered from hay fever. When she refused to recant her faith, she was placed in a room full of

flowers, and flogged herself to death. As is our custom, we didn't take a collection, but charged for tissues.

4th May, Friday
The boys reminded me that it's Star Wars Day, and kept saying 'May the Fourth be with you', and falling about laughing until it was time to go to school. They'll grow out of it, I expect. No jobs worth pursuing in *Church Times* unless I want to be a chaplain in the Royal Navy. One of the team, it says. But I was once sick on the Woolwich Ferry.

Spent the day visiting, because I have sermon-writer's block. It's like ordinary writer's block, but with religious overtones.

5th May, Saturday
Went to the cupboard at the back of the church to get the brush and dustpan to clear up after St Histamine, to avoid the wrath of Mrs Hopkins, and I was overwhelmed by oasis. On examination, it turned out to be the old stuff we threw out last month, not the next generation spawned by the remaining scraps. All very mysterious.

6th May, Fourth Sunday of Easter
Mrs Hooley tried to lighten the mood during the litany by starting a Mexican wave. But nobody else joined in, or, indeed, knew what she was doing.

The crack in the south wall is now so big that

people are using it to sneak out during the sermon. The quinquennial inspection is due anyway, and I have decided to bite the bullet and phone the diocesan architect. It's a bit off-putting when you're preaching about thieves coming in to steal, while people are nipping in and out for a crafty smoke. And it makes locking the church at night a bit of a waste of time.

7th May, Bank Holiday Monday

The Cheeving Morris Men danced in front of the Temporary Sign. Resplendent in white, under colourful rag jackets, they looked like the cricket team on acid. They danced Shooting, Bean Setting, Shepherd's Hey, Tractor Driver's Damn and Artificial Inseminator's Soddit. The Fool pranced around with his bladder on a stick, hitting people with it for good luck. Theirs, presumably, not his, because when Jason Orrell was hit, he laid the Fool out with a straight right, encouraged Lennox to bite him in the flannels, and popped his bladder with his cigarette. Fortunately the bladder in question was a second-hand one, out of a pig, but the thought still makes your eyes water.

A quiet evening in. While Hilary was bathing the boys, I was testing the latest Bulgarian Merlot and watching *Coronation Street*, when an angel appeared unto me, and spake, saying 'Resent!' 'I do,' I told him. 'Angel Delight was unplaced, and your wings are in front of the TV.'

8th May, Tuesday
Chapter meeting. Talk on The Case for the Ciborium, with slides. I thought maybe, but only if you've won the Lottery and your church is the size of Westminster Abbey.

Conversation over coffee took a strange turn, and it seems I am the only member of chapter to have his original wife, a Vauxhall and a prostate gland. But good news from Wilkins, who has managed at last to stop his new curate from jumping up, with stern words and a rolled-up *Church Times*.

I phoned Church House and asked for the diocesan architect. Breathing heavily, he asked when I wanted the fire. I said I wanted a quinquennial inspection, and he said that was a job for the diocesan architect, and put me back to the switchboard. The girl said, 'Sorry, I thought you said arsonist.' An easy enough mistake, I suppose.

9th May, Wednesday
Met Mrs Smallie in the street, beaming all over her face. Her Norman has come back, because the captain of the ladies' darts team can't cook a decent

steak-and-kidney pie, and won't handwash underwear. 'I knew it would work,' said Mrs Smallie. 'Prayer?' I asked. 'No,' she said. 'Putting the oasis back.' I think what this place needs is a mission.

10th May, Thursday

Sensational news from Bishop's Wibbling, where Keith has been suspended after failing a dope test. He completed the mass in 28 minutes, including hymns, and his sample proved positive for several illegal substances, which we thought were only used by sad old clergymen trying to show their bishops they could still cut the mustard. I thought Keith did it all on Kellogg's Special K and strong coffee, but it seems he wasn't just swinging the incense in his thuribles, if you know what I mean. Come to think of it, you probably don't.

11th May, Friday

Like every theology student there ever was, I forgot my Greek as soon as I left college, so imagine my surprise this morning when I answered the door, and there he stood! Large as life, a moustache like a dead rat casting a shadow over his teeth, and the bobbles on his clogs wobbling with emotion. 'Ron!' he cried. 'Iannis?' I said, amazed, and invited him in to talk over old times and catch up with the news. 'I hear you tried to pick up a little Hebrew', he said with a knowing nudge. He was right, but I don't like to be reminded about it, and changed the subject.

12th May, Saturday

I heard the call of the great outdoors. All nature beckoned, and bade me follow. Every twig and leaf, every bud and opening flower summoned me, the song of every bird cried 'Come!' But I still had tomorrow's sermon to write. Life can be tough, sometimes.

13th May, Fifth Sunday of Easter

Jennifer insisted on bringing the Sunday school into church to show us their enactment of the Tower of Babel. I knew it would all end in tears, and I was right. Not that I could take any pleasure in being right, what with a great pile of toddlers all over the chancel step.

Then just because Dennis played something lively at the end of the service, the choir ladies jigged out swinging their hips. I ought to have said something, because apart from being unseemly, a stout chorister swinging her hips in Cheeving Halfpenny probably causes a tornado in Brazil.

14th May, Monday

The Thing in the font has stirred; at any rate, we found a cap and half a pair of glasses in the

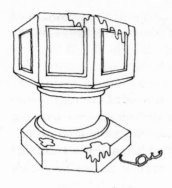

baptistry. Mopped up the slime myself, rather than bother Mrs Hopkins, who always says we should get it seen to. She has no idea what would be involved in getting it seen to, any more than I have.

15th May, Tuesday

The diocesan architect came, and spent ages shaking his head, tutting, and talking into his little tape recorder. Then I persuaded him to stop that, and look at the church. He looked at the outside, the inside, and even climbed up the tower, which is something I try not to do at all. He shouted down over the parapet and asked whether we'd had Zulus camping up there, and I said no, it was a roc's nest. He came down quickly then, looking pale. 'Do they migrate?' he asked, and I said I didn't know, but they flew off, and that was the main thing. Then I asked him what needed doing. He took me to the vestry door, pointed to the bottom hinge, and said, 'I think that might be all right.'

16th May, Wednesday

Old Ted Toomey phoned to ask if he could come and see me, and I said yes, so he turned up with Mrs

Hole, holding her hand, and asked how soon they could get married. And I said three weeks to call the banns, and they both thought they'd live that long. We filled in the form. Edward Toomey, widower, and Todina Hole, widow. Where it said 'age', they both put 'over 21', although I know for a fact Ted is over 85, because we went to his eightieth birthday party, and he sang 'What's new, pussycat?' and everyone was embarrassed but him, and, apparently, Mrs Hole, who realized at that moment that she fancied him something rotten. So I shall call the banns on Sunday. As they left, Ted whispered to me, 'It's all right, Vicar – I haven't got her in trouble!'

17th May, Thursday

Over to Peedle Magna in the evening to see Barney Doors, the new rector, inducted and installed. Officially, he is rector of Peedle Magna, Peedle

Parva, Peedle without the Walls, Great Shakes with Calling All Saints, Huffleigh, Duffleigh, Puffleigh, and Griping St Todger with Pywicket. Fortunately he is the broad-shouldered type who looks like he can bless bricks in

half. Good service, with all
the clergy in the deanery
processing like a flock of
penguins except Harry
Slope, who forgot his kit,
so the bishop made him
do it in his pants and
vest. The chancellor of
the diocese was wearing
a fairly obvious wig. Did
he think we wouldn't notice his own dark hair
sticking out under the white curls? And the little
pigtail wouldn't fool anybody. Very 1970s. The
bishop was his usual august presence, until just as
he reached the chancel step, his mother stepped
out, spat on her hanky and gave him a quick wipe.

Good party afterwards, with vol-au-vents,
cheese and pineapple stuck into half a grapefruit,
little sausages on sticks, and a cake which should
have said, 'Welcome to our new rector' but actually
spelt it with an 'um', which gave us the best laugh
since the bishop got his hand stuck in the alms box.
Say what you like about the Church of England,
but it still puts on a good show.

18th May, Friday
Wedding rehearsal took a turn for the worse when
I said to Martin, 'And now you repeat after me –
look, relax, it's only a rehearsal', and he said, 'Look,
relax, it's only a rehearsal', and we continued

to mine this rich seam of comedy for some time. Martin is only as bright as he has to be to drink chardonnay and be the tennis club secretary. When he was writing me my cheque he asked, 'Do I sign my married name?'

19th May, Saturday
If I'd known how late the bride was going to be, I could have watched *Gone with the Wind*, built a model of a Sopwith Camel or learned Arabic. Sally turned up eventually asking, 'Is Martin here yet?' and I said 'Yes, he's still here, but half the trebles in the choir are now light baritones', but my irony was lost on her. The service itself went smoothly. The best man swayed, but stayed upright, Mrs Things, the bride's mother, cried discreetly, and best of all, the photographer decided not to take any photographs at all afterwards. I had no idea there was a wasps' nest in the church porch until the guard of honour hit it with his tennis racket.

20th May, Sixth Sunday of Easter
Why isn't the past tense of 'preach', 'praught'? I preached on the text 'If you love me, keep my commandments', and reminded everyone that the big board with the ten commandments written on it is there for them all to see at the back of the church. What I didn't remind them is that Amos Screevly, churchwarden, 1845, whose name is the biggest writing on the board, was a serial adulterer, who

served time for embezzlement and put his parents in the workhouse.

Called the banns for Ted Toomey and Todina Hole, daring anyone to object. 'It makes me feel sick just thinking about it' isn't cause or just impediment, and I told Mrs Smallie so.

21st May, Monday
While I was in church, checking for small change down the cracks in the floor, I heard a strange sound. It sounded exactly like hundreds of mice dragging a man-trap, and leaving it outside the vestry door, and baiting it with a copy of *What Candle?* I went to check, and my ears had not deceived me. I grabbed the first thing that came to hand, which was a churchwarden's wand, to spring it. It snapped the wand in two, but I realize I shall have to be careful. I'd been missing that *What Candle?* since before Easter.

22nd May, Tuesday
Transferred the little brass mitre off the top of the churchwarden's wand I broke yesterday on to a broom handle, which was as near the right size as I could find. Colonel Toop won't notice, because the next time he has to process with it will be at the induction of my successor, when I won't care.

A good group at Mrs Jellicle's for Bible study, looking at the book of Jonah. 'We all know the story', I said, and Mrs Jellicle said, 'Yes, he used to be in the *Beano*', which caused a huge digression about who else used to be in the *Beano*. I managed to regain control, and said how like Jonah we all are, because we want God to smite our enemies, rather than forgive them. Mrs Smallie asked, 'Why doesn't God smite a few more sinners?' I said I'm glad he doesn't, because I'd have to be smitten, or smote, or whatever it is, and I'm sure I'd hate it. And whatever Mr Bagg says, Beryl the Peril was in the *Topper*.

23rd May, Wednesday
Took the handle off Hilary's kitchen mop and put it on the church broom, before Mrs Hopkins noticed and made me feel the rough edge of her tongue. Then after the midweek service, I went to see Mrs Smallie, happily handwashing Norman's underwear, with a steak-and-kidney pie in the oven. I noticed there were no umbrellas up indoors, no shoes on the table, and no crossed knives anywhere. And I also noticed her salt pot only has a tiny hole in the top, in case it gets spilled, and there were no ladders at all leaning against the walls of the house. Mrs Smallie must live in a state of superstitious terror.

24th May, Thursday
New people have moved into number 12, and I always think it's good to visit as soon as possible, to show the church is caring. He introduced himself

as Ehud Finkelstein, and his wife as Rebecca, and
he's a retired lawyer from Gants Hill, wherever
that is. They invited me in for tea and a something
called a bagel, and they were absolutely charming,
and showed me pictures of their children and
grandchildren. But as I left, I said, 'Maybe we'll see
you in church one Sunday', and he said, 'I don't
think so.' Was it something I said?

25th May, Friday
I was in the General Store, buying fruit, when Miss
Threadgold crept up on me unawares, caught me
by the grapes and said I really ought to go and see
her. I reminded her that the last time I had called,
she was in no state to receive gentlemen callers.
And she said clergy don't count. According to Miss
Threadgold, clergy are a separate, third gender.

Friday night is fish and chips night. I wish I could
stop the boys playing with their fish, pretending it's
come alive and saying, 'Cod moves in a mysterious
way.' It was funny, once, but laughing was obviously a mistake.

26th May, Saturday
No weddings, and the sermon written, so feeling
very virtuous, I strolled out to watch the cricket,
Cheeving Halfpenny against their deadly rivals,
Calling All Saints. The whole business dates back
to the war, when the people of Calling accused
Cheeving of selling eggs to the Roundheads. So the

bowlers showed no mercy on either side, and balls were hit with incredible violence. Then later, out on the pitch, Cheeving gave Calling a right pasting, with four wickets to spare. And when George, the captain, said it was probably my prayers that did it, I didn't argue, even though all I'd been praying for was a good clean game.

Back to find Hilary holding her mop, and wondering where the handle had got to. 'One of life's little mysteries,' I said, 'Like why I can never find my car keys, and why people confuse pot noodles with food.'

27th May, Sunday

Mrs Smallie didn't turn up, and had. Asked Mr Creek who is her uncle. To read the epistle in her place St Paul. Can be hard to follow at the best. Of times but Charlie Creek raised him. To a whole new level by reading. From his own tiny Bible and treating. The ends of the lines as punctuation the result. Would have been hilarious if I hadn't. Had to preach on it straight away on. The assumption that the congregation. Had at least got the drift of it.

28th May, Monday

I was just picking up the family allowance in the post office, and wondering whether padded envelopes were a bargain if you bought two and got one free, when I bumped into the Brigadier, who said I looked a bit down in the dumps, what? I told him we've got to get the church restored, and it seems like a lot of work, and it's going to cost a lot, and it's weighing on my mind a bit. 'Nothing simpler!' he said. 'Do what I always did. Write "Church will be restored", give it to your ADC, and it gets done.' And there I was, worrying.

29th May, Tuesday

Paprika Bloat and Warren Orrell, Jason's brother, came to see me under cover of darkness, saying they want to get married. As it's only three weeks to the longest day, this meant they fetched up at the vicarage at 9.30, and they've only just gone. Even seeing them together was amazing in itself, as the Bloats and the Orrells tend to hit each other rather than intermarry. But we filled in the forms, and looked through the service, and they've chosen hymns: 'Fight the good fight', 'Through the night of doubt and sorrow' and 'Abide with me', as Warren is Cheeving Halfpenny's official football hooligan. Mrs General has to make special trips to the Cash and Carry just to keep him in toilet rolls.

30th May, Wednesday
Old Mr Starkadder from the farm passed me on his way to the Brethren, nearly knocking me off my bike with his pony and trap. I must start spreading the rumour that knocking a vicar off his bike means seven years' bad luck. I remarked that he seemed to be in a hurry, but he said, without changing his expression, 'They won't start the Quivering without me.' A strange family altogether.

31st May, Thursday
Bumped into Jason Orrell walking Lennox, who was just finishing off a peke. I asked him how he was. 'Vicar,' he said, 'I have decided to accept the Lord Jesus Christ as my personal friend and Saviour.' I said 'No! Really?' and he said 'No. Only joking', and walked off laughing. I never know whether to pray that he sees the light, or falls down a big hole.

June

June

1st June, Friday
No jobs worth pursuing in *Church Times* unless I want to be vicar of a 'challenging' parish in South London. Most of the challenges would be to armed combat, I gather. Anyway, I know people who do inner-city ministry and they look like survivors of the Battle of Inkerman. I'm not saying life in Cheeving Halfpenny isn't real, but at least if I were mugged, I'd know his name.

2nd June, Saturday
Everything coming together for the Patronal Festival on the 17th. No exotic dancer this year, because last time we never found her python before the python found little Jonathan Stebbings, and then we only realized who it was because of his RSCM medallion. I bet Rolf Harris never saw an Indian python operated on to remove a choirboy. So this year, just the jugglers and the Red Chasubles.

3rd June, Pentecost, Whit Sunday

We get more than enough wind through the gaps in the leaded windows, thank you very much, so we just had some good lively hymns, with Dennis at the organ working his elbows like chicken wings, and Adrian preached one of his energetic sermons, his arms flailing like windmill sails, and his family carefully planted in the congregation, urging him on and shouting 'Halleluia!' Am I the only one who stands still while I worship? Maybe if I stood at the altar and pretended to be conducting Beethoven's Ninth, people would say I had charisma, but most likely I'd just knock everything over. At lunch, the boys did their impression of Adrian preaching, and custard went everywhere.

4th June, Monday

The trouble with those stoles some clergy wear at Pentecost, with the symbolic flames embroidered at the bottom, is that if they do catch fire, nobody takes any notice. Wilkins phoned to tell me that his

curate was treated at the vet's as an out-patient, but hopes the young scamp will have learned a lesson. No chance. Wilkins' curate is a disaster waiting to happen. When he was ordained, several priests who laid hands on him claimed to have had electric shocks.

5th June, Tuesday
A strange invitation in the post – tea next month with someone I'd never heard of. I showed it to Hilary, and said 'I don't know anyone called Sidney Blicester.' And she said, 'Yes you do – the bishop.' Silly me.

6th June, Wednesday
Little Damian is excused assembly at school because he is the Antichrist, and has to sit in Room 3 with Sean, Kevin, Seamus, Finbar, Eammon, Malachy, Katy, Siobhan, Mary and Shelagh the Roman Catholics and Molly the Jehovah's Witness. Damian would be a more loveable child if he smiled more and hissed less.

7th June, Thursday
Came back from a morning's visiting, full of tea, to find the vicarage drive, and access to the loo, blocked by a huge van, manoeuvring down backwards, because it was too big to turn around at the top. Branches snapped from the trees, stones were knocked from the walls, tempers frayed, but at last the leviathan was back on the road and heading down the High Street, where it met the bus from Blicester coming the other way, and I wish I'd had time to watch the ensuing stand-off.

I wondered what Hilary had been spending my stipend on. I was expecting to see a three-piece suite, or a double wardrobe, or at the very least a chest freezer. It was the diocesan architect's report.

8th June, Friday
The architect's report is the size of Marlon Brando and will cost us as much, as the architect is on 10 per cent, and the total cost of the work needed is about the same as a house in the country with extensive outbuildings and views over the South Downs, or David Beckham's wages for a week.

9th June, Saturday
Sat down with a big mug of coffee and the architect's report. It confirms something I've always suspected. People have often remarked how big the church is inside, and now it's official. The church is six feet longer inside than it is outside, a feat of medieval building not repeated anywhere else as far as is known, and preserved by the Victorians who restored the church in 1875.

In the afternoon, Edward Toomey and Todina Hole were married. Only Hilary, and Dennis Elbeau, who had come up anyway to practice for tomorrow, were there as witnesses. After the Blessing, Ted said, 'Go on, Vicar, say it.' 'Say what?' I asked. 'You may kiss the bride', he said, with a horrible leer. So I said it. And Mrs Hole smiled, took her handkerchief from her pocket, and took her teeth out into it.

10th June, Trinity Sunday

Cries of disbelief when I called Paprika Bloat and Warren Orrell's banns. Nothing like it has happened in the village before. It will go down in the annals with the Great Stink of 1878 and the Day the Goat Got Out.

Note for next year: juggling three balls to illustrate the doctrine of the Holy Trinity is only a good idea if you can actually juggle.

11th June, Monday

Hilary keeps asking how long the architect's report is going to be in the study, as it blocks out most of the light. I've tried skimming through it, but it's like skimming through the dictionary and trying to work out the plot.

12th June, Tuesday

Chapter meeting. Barney Doors, being the new boy, had his cap thrown on to the bicycle-shed roof, his head held down the toilet, and given a thorough flicking with wet corporals, which is not as labour-intensive as it sounds. Then to business – a talk on Monstrances, with colour slides. I'm afraid we all got the giggles, and started doing jokes about Frankenstein's Monstrance, the Loch Ness Monstrance and those silver ones with little windows in and the gilt twiddly bits.

The boys have built a den in the architect's report, and insist on eating their meals there, pretending to be outlaws.

13th June, Wednesday
Meeting of PCC. All present except Mrs Hope, who sent her apologies because she has blackfly. I broke the news about the building repairs, and Colonel Toop immediately suggested we hijack a bulldozer, knock the building down and claim on the insurance. I was shocked and scandalized that he should suggest such a course of action, and besides, a bulldozer wouldn't go through the lychgate. Miss Tredgett suggested we get somebody really old to change their will. She is 85, and we all looked at her and she said, 'I have my cats to think of', and went quiet. Mrs Thomas asked whether I might sell some indulgences. Finally the treasurer, Harry Parry, coughed and said this might be a good time for him to give his financial report. He stood up, straightened his tie, produced a small piece of paper said, 'We're broke', and sat down again. I reminded everyone of the fête on the 23rd, and Harry said we could have a fête once a month and we'd still be broke. I decided I needed a drink.

Arthur down at the Temporary Sign said, 'There's gypsies camping on Upwood Green', and my heart sank. Every year when the gypsies come for the radish-thinning, there is an outbreak of thieving and petty pilfering, and worse trouble sometimes follows. I shall go to Upwood Green in the morning.

14th June, Thursday

My worst fears are confirmed. The gypsy caravan was propped up on bricks, because the wheels had been stolen, and Abel Petulengro was holding the horse by the mane because someone had taken its bridle. The wheels will no doubt be in someone's garden by now being a 'Feature', but why anyone would want the bridle is beyond me. I always said Cheeving would be a one-horse town if anyone had a horse. Sympathized with Abel and his family who have also lost the battery from their lorry, and all the children's wellingtons left outside the caravan. 'Yer a bunch of thievin' b*****ds,' said Abel, 'who don't deserve any good luck.' I stood there looking contrite, and asked him if he had any lucky heather to sell me, hoping he wouldn't curse the village. The last time he did that, when they'd even had the washing taken from the lines, there were so many slugs the village street was all but impassable, and salad prices shot through the roof.

15th June, Friday

Rained frogs.

16th June, Saturday

I was sitting outside the Temporary Sign, enjoying a pint of Busticle's, when Wilkins turned up, wearing sandals and socks, which immediately marks him as an off-duty clergyman. He says Saturday is his day off, which is strange, because no vicar ever does anything on Saturday anyway unless there's a wedding. He was grumbling about his curate, who is recovering nicely, and I said I wouldn't mind one. 'They're a tie,' he said. 'You can't go off anywhere unless you find someone willing to look after them; if you have them neutered they get fat, and if you don't, every girl in the parish comes howling on your doorstep, and they leave muddy footprints everywhere.' I asked him where his came from, and he said from a refuge. His last parish had treated him badly, and if he hadn't taken him in, he would have had to be put down. I said, 'But he comes in handy at Christmas, doesn't he?' Wilkins nearly choked on his beer. 'Everyone says that,' he said, 'But a curate isn't just for Christmas, it's for life.'

17th June, First Sunday after Trinity, St Gargoyle's Day

The Red Chasubles performed in tight formation, thrilling the crowds with their near-miss passes and death-defying feats of skill. When the two files split, and crossed through each other, a spontaneous ripple of applause passed through the assembled multitude, and when they swung their thuribles in perfect unison, sending plumes of coloured smoke skyward, there was an audible gasp of admiration. The juggler was a bit of a disappointment after that, so it was up to me in my sermon to enthuse the congregation. St Gargoyle is the patron saint of nightclub bouncers, lollipop ladies, basket weavers and washing machine service engineers, and tying that in with a passage from Leviticus about how to deal with mould was a real challenge, but I think I rose to it. Tea was served in the hall. Big Colin, the doorman at Uncle Joe's nightclub in Blicester, came to the service in his dinner jacket and dark glasses, his head impeccably shaved. He sidled up to me, and said in a conspiratorial whisper, 'I made a basket, once', which goes to show you never can tell.

18th June, Monday

I spent the day driving around the Peedles, and the surrounding villages, sticking up posters for the fête. I was horrified to see how many of Barney's parishes have fêtes the same day as ours, so I had to put our poster over theirs. Anyway, theirs are just fêtes, and ours is a Grand Fête.

19th June, Tuesday

The vicarage is filling up with stuff for the fête. This happens every year, as soon as the Patronal Festival is over. Hilary says we ought to make St Gargoyle's day a fundraiser, and maybe she has a point. The boys looked at a heap of boxes in the hallway, bulging with rupture trusses, chest expanders, basketball hoops and bagpipes, and asked what it all was. I said it was white elephants, and they looked at me as though I'd just confirmed their suspicion that all grown-ups are mad. And there is a growing jam mountain in the kitchen that Hilary treats as a sort of roundabout, and I really do have a lovely bunch of coconuts, which will play an important part in some game of skill, I'm told.

Looked at Micah at Bible study. Somebody said that the bit about Bethlehem always made her feel Christmassy. I pointed out that Thursday is the longest day. Mrs Jellicle said if anyone wanted a mince pie, she was sure she could find some.

20th June, Wednesday
An angel sat here works these ills.

21st June, Thursday
Apparently the person at Church House who advises on fundraising is Mr Donald Capelletti. He wasn't in, so I'll call back tomorrow.

Hilary insists that the freezer is full of cakes because it's the fête on Saturday and there is a cake stall, in case I hadn't noticed. And she's counted them. Which is bad news for me and the boys. We've already eaten half of one.

22nd June, Friday
Asked to speak to the diocesan fundraiser. A familiar voice breathed heavily down the phone, and asked, 'When do you want the fire?' The girl on the switchboard apologized and said, 'I thought you

wanted the diocesan fire-raiser.' I asked if she was hard of hearing, and she said, 'No, I'm eating melon.'

The diocesan fundraising adviser is actually called Don Capelletti, a gentleman of the Italian persuasion. He says yes, we can raise funds, and he thinks I will find his terms very reasonable, whatever that means. I told him we have our church fête tomorrow, one of the high spots of the social calendar, and usually good for a few hundred quid, and he said, 'I'm talking funds here. Real money. Enjoy your fête.'

23rd June, Saturday

A glorious day for the fête, and everyone seemed to be up at first light hanging bunting, setting up stalls, all ignoring Joan's carefully drawn up plan, and putting their stalls where they do every year, just because. The steam organ arrived, and started playing 'What a friend we have in Jesus', and I teased Dennis about how he'd have to be careful I didn't get one instead of him. It then played 'I've got a lovely bunch of coconuts', and Dennis said if I want him to play that, I only have to ask.

The bouncy castle never turned up, so there was a bit of a gap in the ground plan. We charged children 50p to jump up and down in the space and use their imaginations, but it's not the same, is it? The fête was opened by the chap who does the cartoons in *Church Times*, but as the only one in

the village who reads it is me, nobody had a clue who he was. And he didn't take his hand out of his pocket as often as I'd have liked. Mrs Pryke's chocolate brownies with herbs in sold out before I had a chance to try one, and when I asked what they were like, people just giggled, which was odd. The top prize on the Pick a Straw was a bottle of Scotch, and when there were only a dozen straws left, and the prize unclaimed, Norman Smallie came forward, bought the lot and secured himself a bargain, and a can of Fanta as well.

Terry Vile was selling helium balloons, and when he wanted to visit the tea tent, he handed the lot to Rupert Stebbings, and said, 'Hold these for a minute.' He should have borne in mind that Rupert Stebbings is very small.

24th June, Second Sunday after Trinity

Harry Parry has done some rough calculations, and bearing in mind floats and expenses still have to be subtracted, he told me I could tell the congregation confidently that yesterday's effort raised enough to cover the faculty application, with maybe enough left over to buy the linseed oil for the church door.

25th June, Monday

I always tell people who ask that a faculty is the Church's version of planning permission. The application is like an income tax form – huge and forbidding, like Colditz Castle in a brown envelope. I kept finding things to do instead of filling it in, like making coffee, cutting the grass, and seeing how long I could suck a polo mint without it breaking. Hilary came back from her computer animation lesson and caught me muttering about how this had nothing to do with the kingdom of God, but she stood over me until it was done. All I need now is a cheque from Harry Parry and it can go off to Church House. Even more bad news for me and the boys. Hilary has found the half cake.

26th June, Tuesday

Harry Parry wrote me a cheque to send with the faculty application, and then he needed extensive counselling. Wait till he has to pay for the actual works. He'll need a solemn mass and hypnotherapy.

We have to get three separate tenders from builders to do the work on the church. And the archdeacon warned us against employing cowboys. So I've told Joan the PCC secretary to write to respectable local firms: Ike Clanton and Sons, the James Brothers, and Roy, Rogers and Trigger.

27th June, Wednesday

As I walked past Old Len's cottage, there he was in his garden, hoeing between immaculate rows of vegetables. I stopped to admire, and we did the joke about how it looked when God had it all to himself, and then he leaned on his hoe and said, 'Do you like strawberries, Vicar?' and I said I did. He went off and came back with two large punnets full. 'And what about raspberries?' he asked, and presented me with two punnets of raspberries, too. I thanked him very much, and he said, 'That'll be £4.50, then.'

28th June, Thursday
Tragedy at the Temporary Sign. The village is stunned by the shock, or it will be when the news gets around. Doris was down in the cellar changing a barrel of Danish lager when it exploded. Doctor Kelly was called, and arrived at warp factor nine, because the words, 'You're needed at the pub' made him break the laws of physics. He came back up from the cellar in a state of shock. Not only was Doris dead, he pronounced, but Doris was a man. None more surprised than Jason Orrell, who turned very pale, left his pint unfinished, an event in itself unheard of, and walked out. Which is a pity, because as Doctor Kelly's breath had stopped the pub clock, he could have stayed all night.

June

29th June, Friday
Don Capelletti telephoned. 'Acts chapter five', he said. 'Pardon?' I said. 'Acts chapter five,' he repeated, 'Ananias and Sapphira. Sunday morning, you tell them.' And he put the phone down.

30th June, Saturday
Three men in overalls wandering about in the churchyard, so I went out to see them. 'Are you looking for something?' I asked, and the biggest one said, 'Yes, the church.' I pointed it out through the thickets, looking like the Sleeping Beauty's castle. The three introduced themselves as Roger Roy, Roy Rogers, and Big Dave Trigger, and said they'd come to look at the job before putting in their tender. As I only posted the letters on Tuesday, I was impressed by their keenness. They asked who else I'd been in touch with, and when I told them, Big Dave curled his lip impressively, and said 'Bunch of cowboys!'

A truck laboured up the vicarage drive, always a tricky operation, and one of the main reasons I stay in this parish, because moving would be a logistical nightmare. In any contest between the truck and the wall, the truck seems to come off worst. Once at the top, the driver got out, looked at the scratches down the side, threw his cap at them and said a word. Then he saw me, apologized, and said, 'Where do you want the bouncy castle?'

July

July

1st July, Third Sunday after Trinity

I put out a plea for volunteers to help clear the churchyard next weekend. There have been the usual complaints from people who can't find their grannies' graves, which always happens; but this year, the people in Glebe Close have seen a strange ape-like creature going through their dustbins, and running back into the thickets, and they're threatening a petition to the archdeacon, which I could do without. I think the archdeacon has forgotten I'm here, and I don't want to remind him.

2nd July, Monday

Doris' parents came to see me, and confirmed that he was indeed called Donald really, and said, 'It's a long story, Padre.' It certainly was, and I now have to do a funeral for Donald, his parents' only son, who everyone knew as Doris, their favourite barmaid, who served drinks, engaged in cheerful banter, and could meet physical violence with the strength and skill of an American wrestler. And we all thought those biceps were the result of pulling pints.

3rd July, Tuesday

A loud thud from the dining room about 2 o'clock. A cherub had hit the window at speed, probably attracted by the Marmite jar still on the table after lunch. What is it about cherubs and Marmite? Fortunately, nothing was broken. We found the poor little chap on the patio, stunned. However, he soon recovered and flew off, but left a perfect impression on the glass, arms and legs spread out, even the surprised expression on his little face. I took a photo. If it comes out, I'll use it as a Christmas card.

4th July, Wednesday

Ike Clanton, the builder, came to look at the church. He wandered around outside saying, 'OK, OK' to himself, and I excused myself while I took the midweek service. He came in halfway through said, 'Don't mind me', and generally carried on as if we weren't there. Actually, apart from me, Colonel Toop and Mrs Hope, we weren't there.

5th July, Thursday

Don Capelletti called. 'Did you do it?' he asked, in his husky Italian accent. 'Did you tell them what happened to Ananias?' I said that the reading had been about the apostles being given authority, and it was hard to work in God striking liars dead. 'You disappoint me,' he said. 'There are two ways to do this. My way', he said, and then added, with a hint of menace in his voice, 'Or a thermometer.' 'A what?' I asked. 'You know,' he said. 'Outside the church. Very tacky. We must meet.' I agreed he could come Friday week. The alternative seemed to be burial under a motorway.

6th July, Friday

Doris' funeral was a masterpiece of tact and diplomacy, if I say so myself. I used the names Doris and Donald alternately. Jason Orrell was conspicuous by his absence. Henry Dolt had had the brass plate inscribed 'Donald Fisk (Doris)' which I thought was quite tasteful, although every time I do a funeral now I'm on tenterhooks, wondering what he will do wrong, and at which point in the proceedings the blow will fall. This time, he left it until the very last minute, standing at the graveside with his handful of soil, and as I read the committal, the edge subsided, and he descended, still standing upright, on the avalanche that covered the coffin. His expletive was so quiet, most people didn't even hear it.

No jobs worth pursuing in *Church Times* unless I want to be chaplain to Ursula Andress' former husbands. But I could do with fewer souls to look after, not more.

7th July, Saturday

The churchyard working party set up a base camp at the lychgate, leaving their faithful servant guarding the heavy equipment. Then, after standing bareheaded a moment, commending themselves to a Higher Power, they set off, followed by a procession of bearers with the food, water, and a plentiful supply of beads and looking-glasses. The noise of their strimmers grew more distant, until only the smoke from their two-strokes betrayed their presence at all.

8th July, Fourth Sunday after Trinity
I was absolutely fascinated
by the sight of a lot of
ants struggling with
something many
times their own
weight. I could have
watched them for
hours, as they heaved with all their strength, slowly
dragging this enormous burden towards their nest.
But instead, I finished my sermon, and asked the
sidesmen to rescue Miss Tredgett. Something must
be done about those ants.

9th July, Monday
As I sat on the verandah, listening to the incessant
scritch of the crickets, swatting flies and trying to
pretend a small gin and tonic was larger, I saw a
strange figure approaching from the west, staggering, and sometimes falling, before struggling to his
feet again. As he collapsed finally in front of me, I
recognized him, despite his ragged clothes and
emaciated limbs, as one of the churchyard working
party, his unshaved cheeks sunken, and his eyes
bright with fever. I gave the poor wretch some
water, which he drank greedily, and then babbled
something about having found the Lost Tomb of

Lemuel Heaves, which no white man has seen for nearly 300 years. Then he became insensible. Can this be true?

10th July, Tuesday
Chapter meeting. Talk on Holy Water, and the Use of the Aspergillum. Just as he was saying that not everyone is comfortable being sprinkled with holy water, Canon Hubble sneezed into his coffee. Not everyone was comfortable being sprinkled with warm coffee either, and we didn't know whether to say 'Bless you' or whether he'd just blessed us.

11th July, Wednesday
Survivors of the churchyard working party staggered back, mere shadows of their former selves, and all shaking their heads when asked about their experiences in the interior. One day, perhaps, the full story will be told.

12th July, Thursday
Ray offered me an anteater to deal with the ants in the church. 'There's your scaly,' he said, 'What we in the trade calls a Pangolin', and while I was considering this strange creature, like a pine cone on legs, he went on, 'Or there's your giant, which is a proper edentate and comes in snazzy black and white.'

It certainly looked an impressive animal, and before I knew what was happening, Ray was saying 'You won't regret this, Vicar', and shaking my hand vigorously.

13th July, Friday

Fortunately, I'm not superstitious, touch wood. Don Capelletti arrived in a dark chalk-stripe suit, dark glasses and a broad-brimmed hat. He looked at our crumbling masonry, and said, 'You wouldn't want any . . . *accidents*', and made it sound like a threat. Broadly speaking, his strategy for fundraising is simple. 'You know who has money,' he said, 'You ask them for it. And don't forget Ananias.' He asked how much we needed to raise, and I told him. He didn't fall off his chair, which was what I did when I was first told. 'Think of it,' he said. 'A jumble sale every week for the next ten years. Will that bring honour to God? Or a thermometer. No. Go to your people and ask.'

14th July, Saturday

While I was in the General Store, stocking up on washing tongs, Vaseline and anchovy fillets, Mrs McSporran sidled up to me and suggested we have a flower festival to raise funds. I said we had one last year, and she said, 'No, Vicar, a Flour Festival. Self-raising, wholemeal, gluten free – the possibilities are manifold.' Mrs McSporran talks like Miss Jean Brodie. I said I didn't think people would pay to see a lot of flour, and she said, 'That's the clever bit, Vicar! They'll think you can't spell, and they won't know until they've paid!' She poked me with her baguette and said, 'Give it some thought!'

15th July, Fifth Sunday after Trinity
Annual Blessing of the Gnomes.
The retired banker at Dunrobin
has so many now I just blessed
his garden hose and left him to it.

16th July, Monday
I hate it when someone phones and says, 'I know it's your day off, Vicar, but . . .' only in this case it was Ray, saying the anteater has come. He brought it round in the van, and we took it into the church straight away. It immediately started licking up ants with a tongue a foot long, obviously quite at home. Ray said, 'Have you thought about names?' and I said, 'No, I just call them The Ants'. 'Alice would be good,' he said, 'it alliterates.' I said, 'That's all right. If it does, Mrs Hopkins will clean it up.'

17th July, Tuesday
I know Ken at the garage has money, because he's got quite a bit of mine, so I went to see him to get a donation for the restoration fund, just like Don Capelletti said. We sat in his tiny office, where everything is black and oily, and he made me a mug

of tea, which was black and oily, too. Even the girls on the calendar on the wall were, well, never mind. I told him why I'd come, and he said times were hard, which I suppose is why he drives a Daimler, and business is slack, which must be why he can't fit in a service before September, after his holiday in the Seychelles. I thought maybe I could offer to spread the word, and recommend him to other people, in return for any generosity he might show, so I said, 'I could tell people about you', and he went pale. 'There's nothing in it,' he said. 'We only play Scrabble. Her husband is in the SAS and he can't even spell that.' And while I sat there wondering what to say, he wrote me a four-figure cheque.

18th July, Wednesday

Don't you just hate it when those little green demons that smell of bassoons poke you with their forks and accuse you of stealing their yoghurt? Hilary not best pleased having to clean the kitchen up afterwards. I need my holiday.

19th July, Thursday

Very odd. In the churchyard, there was a young clergyman, impeccably dressed, and when I approached him he said, 'Ah! Here come the others!' and offered me his hand. But it wasn't the official handshake they teach you when you're ordained –

this was a lay person pretending! 'What others?' I asked him. 'Aren't you with Van Wipples?' he asked, 'Here for the photo-shoot?' I demanded an explanation, but before he could start, a whole bunch of bogus clergy arrived, with a photographer, and trunks full of vestments, shirts, clerical boxer shorts and pyjamas. The photographer looked me up and down and said, 'You can push off – I'm not doing before and after.'

20th July, Friday

Joan, the PCC secretary, was heavily bribed to sit with the boys while Hilary and I set off for tea at the bishop's palace. I thought it would be cosy and intimate, just the three of us, but there were about 60 clergy and their wives all milling about, drinking tea and eating cucumber sandwiches, scones and Victoria sponge. As it was a nice day we were led outside, where a peacock immediately ate my scone. Hilary looked lovely in her posh frock, making all the other vicars' wives look dowdy. Considering how hot it was, you wonder what it would take to get some of them out of thick tweed and lisle stockings. The only sour note was struck when the Vicar of Hugely inadvertently tapped out his pipe on the bishop's tortoise, without realizing that Bishop Sidney once boxed for the army. Fortunately, he never saw what I did to the peacock.

21st July, Saturday

Paprika and Warren's wedding day. The day dark and threatening, and the weather, too. The ushers were seven feet tall, built like brick outhouses in dark glasses, and insisted that the bride's family kept to the left side of the church, and the Orrells sat on the right. They assumed, rightly, that they had no friends in common. The two sides competed singing the hymns, not to sing louder, but faster, so 'Fight the good fight' was sung at the speed of 'The flight of the bumble-bee'. Paprika's vows were accompanied by subdued hissing from the Orrells, like a hedgehog in a bouncy castle, and Warren had to shout his vows above booing from the Bloat pews. Paprika's father and Jason Orrell scuffled for the pen to sign the register first. Arthur Bloat won, and wrote his name so large that Jason had to squeeze his in tiny, and there wasn't room for mine at all. Outside in the churchyard it looked like *West Side Story*, and I was glad to slip away. I had to pick my way between little clumps of Bloat children, all wearing lurid waistcoats like scale models of snooker players, scowling across the churchyard at the young Orrells, who were chanting, 'Come over here if you think you're hard enough.' 'You're coming to the reception, aren't you, Vicar?' shouted Arthur Bloat, and I said I'd love to, but I had to arrange my coloured pencils into alphabetical order.

22nd July, Sixth Sunday after Trinity, St Nobby of Kirkburton

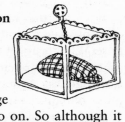

Bad night, and little sleep. Sirens through the village all night as the emergency services tried to cope with the wedding reception at the village hall. But normal life has to go on. So although it was tipping with traditional Nobbytide rain, St Nobby's cap, in its reliquary, the glass sparkling and the cushion freshly hoovered, was taken from the church, and carried in solemn procession, preceded by the crucifer, the choir singing 'Ee, St Nobby', and with the congregation following behind, carrying her umbrella. As usual, in the lane, we met the procession from Cheeving Parva coming the other way, with their own so-called Cap of St Nobby, in it's reliquary. How anyone could believe that St Nobby would have worn felt is beyond me. Ours, the authentic cap, is made of tweed. Neither procession would give way, so there was some ill-natured elbowing as they passed. But then, ill-natured elbowing was very much a part of St Nobby's earthly life in Yorkshire.

23rd July, Monday

A letter arrived from Van Wipples, asking permission to use the churchyard for a catalogue photoshoot. It was dated 5 May, but a snail had eaten the postcode. I noticed there was no mention of payment.

The village hall is now a smouldering ruin – heavy rain did nothing to prevent its ancient, alcohol-soaked timbers from burning fiercely. A miserable group of villagers stood looking at the ashes. Stories are circulating of heroic deeds done that night, as Arthur Bloat organized the children into a human chain to save the beer, passing bottles of Busticle's Odd Peculiar from hand to hand, and Jason Orrell had to be restrained from dashing back into the inferno to rescue the dartboard. There are conflicting stories as to how it started. The most likely is that somebody's cigarette set their drink on fire. The least likely is that God thought the party was getting out of hand, and smote it with brimstone.

Weather still awful, considering it's nearly August, and we're off on holiday at the weekend. Much prayer is called for.

24th July, Tuesday
Bible study on Nahum. As all Nahum does is propose three cheers for the fall of Nineveh, thus providing a sort of three-dimensional jigsaw for archaeologists, it wasn't a very long meeting.

25th July, Wednesday
I went to see Mrs General at the Stores, to solicit a donation for the restoration fund. She was improving the shining hour by peeling the little labels off Moroccan oranges, and putting them in a box marked 'Locally Grown'. Mrs General does very

well out of the people who haven't got cars to go to the supermarkets in Blicester, and she's usually good for a raffle prize at the fête and the bazaar. And to show I could repay any generosity she might show, by recommending the Stores to people, I said, 'I could tell everybody all about you.' Mrs General went pale and flustered, and said, 'He's a poor soldier whose wife doesn't give him the time of day! Just because he's in the SAS, and has a cheesewire in his top pocket, she thinks he's not sensitive!' And she wrote me a four-figure cheque.

26th July, Thursday
I called on Harry Parry, who was watering his hanging baskets, and his face fell when he saw me coming. But when I gave him the cheques from Ken at the garage and Mrs General, something like a smile spread over the front of his head. I say something like a smile, because no church treasurer can ever be really happy. If Harry didn't have his hanging baskets, I believe he'd have thrown himself under Jason's dog long ago.

I'm getting quite excited about my holiday, and took my shorts out to try on. Hilary saw me and fell about laughing. I'm sure I don't know why, and her remarks about Desert Rats were quite uncalled for. I said I intended to wear them on the beach, and she said, 'Good – we needn't take a windbreak. Or a sunshade.'

27th July, Friday

I handed the church keys to the Colonel, asking him to make sure he fed Alice the anteater. 'Jolly good,' he said. 'What does she eat?' I phoned Eric, the retired priest who lives in Griping St Todger, to make sure he was all right for Sunday, and he called me Dear Boy, and assured me everything would be wonderful, and he was looking forward to it, as it would be the first time he'd done the full mass in Latin. He must have heard me boggling, because he said, 'Didn't you know? I went to Rome when they started ordaining . . . what was it? Zebras? Orang-utans? Oh, yes, I remember, women!' If he wasn't joking, it's too late anyway. Poor Eric. He's been retired years, and still occasionally forgets himself, and drinks the washing-up water. Prayed for fine weather.

28th July, Saturday

Holiday! The boys were up at first light, and their idea of packing is to heap up everything they possess except clothes, but eventually, we managed to whittle them down to a caseful each, and set off south for the coast. They started asking, 'Are we there yet?' before we'd passed the church. We stopped for necessary reasons at the village of Mound, and to see the mound which is all that is left of the castle. I'd told the boys about it, and they seemed quite excited. Sir Rydal Schyvinge went off to fight the crusades, leaving a stone castle in the middle of a wattle-and-daub village, and when he came back, there was a stone village and no castle at all, the serfs having stolen it. The parish church of St Barry would be gloomy enough, but it has medieval murals of skeletons everywhere, with scrolls saying things like 'Prepare ye to followe mee', 'I am thy due' and 'I once ette a pot noodle'. I could imagine the painter thinking he'd really brightened the place up. As we got back in the car, the boys asked, 'When are we going to see the mound?' and I said that was it, that little hill thing. I asked what they expected a mound to be like, and they said, 'Maybe more like a dragon.'

Arrived at Swanmouth in time for lunch, and unpacked. I'm sure I put my shorts in, but there was no sign of them. We found that the boys had packed again after us, replacing all their clothes with toys, which means they will either be kitted out in new clothes we can't afford, or very smelly by the end of the week. Weather gorgeous. So there is a God.

29th July, Seventh Sunday after Trinity
Went to church in Swanmouth. Higher than we're used to, but modern, so although they use incense, it comes as a handy aerosol. We noticed more than one member of the congregation checking his armpits as they were given their squirt. Then the epistle was just being read, from a lectern shaped like the Starship Enterprise, with Paul telling Timothy that a church leader ought to be able to

control his family, when the
boys started to fight, trading
blows despite everything I
could do to keep them
apart. Lucky I wasn't
wearing a dog collar.

Professor Pilchard's
Punch and Judy had some
nice modern touches, too,
with the health inspector confiscating the sausages,
the baby phoning Childline, and a new character
who introduced himself as Judy's lawyer.

Getting the boys ready for bed, we found their
pockets full of sticky pink goo, which they protested
was candy floss they were saving for later. Fortunately, the hotel has a bar.

30th July, Monday

Professor Pilchard was taking Mr Punch for a
promotional walk along the promenade, and the
boys saw him, and their bottom lips trembled as
they wailed, 'It's a puppet!' and refused to be con-
soled until we'd bought them 99s. When they find
out the truth about Father Christmas, I'll probably
have to buy them a gallon tub.

In the evening, we found they'd filled their suit-
case with sand. They said it was sand castle kits,
and they were going to sell them back home and
make money. What funny little chaps they are.

31st July, Tuesday

Don't ask. Just don't ask.

August

1st August, Wednesday

The boys spent the day building huge gothic edifices in the sand, decorated with sea shells and ice lolly sticks. And after yesterday's episode, I left the car keys in our room. It was an expensive business, and the boys seemed to think that 'In the sand' was all the answer 'Where are my keys?' required. Hilary felt the need for some retail therapy, and took  herself off to the shops, while I sat in a deckchair, reading the latest thriller from Canterbury Press, pondering on the wonders of creation, and refereeing when the boys came to blows. When I see God, I must ask him why dogs come out of the sea, ignore their owners and come and shake all over me. That's after I've asked him about the slugs, and why the wonders of creation poo on my hat. Hilary came back to report that Swanmouth has exactly the same shops as Blicester, in exactly the same order. But she did get me a nice pair of shorts.

I'm quite looking forward to getting home so I can eat something that isn't fried.

2nd August, Thursday
The boys took to the water on their inflatable tortoise, and although they both swim like fish, I'm convinced only constant prayers to St Nicholas, the patron of children and sailors, prevented a disaster. The weather was so warm I was tempted to get in as well, and Hilary assured me the shorts  wouldn't suffer from getting wet. But the boys showed me how they could dive, and before I knew what was happening, I had no shorts, and the tortoise had a sail. So I had to stay in water up to my chest while negotiations went on. Regaining my dignity cost me a family bucket of fried chicken and chips. Why would anybody choose to eat out of a bucket?

3rd August, Friday
I thought a nice walk might be a good way to round off our holiday, and supposed that nothing much could go wrong on a nice walk. This was a mistake, as the boys narrowly escaped being shot for sheep-worrying, claimed to have found a pirate's treasure, except he wasn't a pirate, and a wallet isn't treasure, and the snake they wanted to take home as a pet was an adder. On the whole, it seemed safer to let them go to the arcade, which was what they

wanted to do all along, and somehow they managed to win a soft toy so ugly it looked like a
gargoyle made of yellow plush.

Once they were clean and in bed, Hilary and I
tried to relax in the bar, but we noticed that in
discussing the boys, we both referred to them as
'your children'.

4th August, Saturday
Home to find the answering machine had been left
on and there were 115 messages. My finger slipped
and I erased the lot. How clumsy of me. And Alice
the anteater has had puppies, or kittens, or whatever
you call baby anteaters. The boys think they're
cute, which is true up to a point, the point where
they lick you with tongues longer than themselves.

5th August, Eighth Sunday after Trinity
I can't believe I fell for the whoopee hassock again.
That's four times this year, not including 1 April,
when it's almost a tradition. Short of sending in an
unmanned probe before I kneel in my stall, I don't
see what I can do about it, and it makes me look
silly in front of the choir. The woodworm in the
pulpit is so bad I have to shout to make myself
heard over the sound of chewing. One day I shall
fall through, and land in the crypt. And I swear that
when we sang 'Onward, Christian Soldiers' they
picked up the rhythm and were munching in time.
Any hopes that anteaters might eat woodworm are

dashed. They can tell the difference, and they're picky.

6th August, Monday

Another builder came to look at the church and estimate for the work. He introduced himself as Frank James, and said his brother couldn't come because he was hanging a picture, and when Jesse hangs a picture, it might take a while, but that picture stays hung. He referred to the anteater as an 'ornery critter', tapped his teeth with a pencil until I had to go away and leave him alone, and when I came back, he said he was just off, and I'd be hearing from him.

7th August, Tuesday

The photocopier has started eating paper, and lighting up little messages to say so. I tried poking about inside, while Hilary stood there saying, 'Call the man out' over and over again. I took out all the bits you're allowed to take out, and all the half chewed bits of sooty paper, but it still refused to copy anything. So I called the man out.

8th August, Wednesday

The photocopier man came, carrying one of those shiny metal cases that usually contain nuclear bombs in James Bond films. He said the feed pinch-roller was knackered, noticed my collar and asked me to pardon his French, and fitted a new one.

Hilary made him tea and chatted to him while I got on with the serious business of the hymn list for September. If the choir don't have it by tomorrow, they will make their displeasure felt.

9th August, Thursday
Cups of tea: 6
Our Fathers: 4
People asking 'Is it hot enough for you, Vicar?': 1
There are posters on the trees and telegraph poles in the village with pictures of Wilkins' curate, who is missing. Poor Wilkins is distraught, as he didn't come home on Monday, and he never misses *The Simpsons*. Wilkins has visions of him lying injured somewhere, or trapped in a shed. But surely he couldn't have come as far as Cheeving? It's a good 12 miles across country, and there are main roads to cross.

10th August, Friday
So hot, I stopped for a mid-day pint of Busticle's at the Temporary sign. P582XAA came to join me, and I greeted him with a cheerful 'Hello, P!' He smiled broadly, pointed to a shiny new car parked across the road, and said, 'I've gone upmarket – just call me W433LJH.' He asked, 'Do you bless cars?' and I told him I haven't yet, but if an army chaplain can bless a tank, I'm sure I can bless a car, and he's going to bring it up the drive a week today.

I spent the evening putting together the service

for Sunday. I doubt if I'll have time tomorrow. Lots of readings about Moses' staff turning into a snake, Jonathan sticking his rod into a honeycomb, and Psalm 23, because of the bit about having a rod and a staff to comfort me. I think about it whenever I go to Ferret's Bottom. A big stick would comfort me, too.

11th August, Saturday

The annual choir outing. On the grounds that anyone whose voice has broken probably thinks Cliché Theme Park is deeply uncool, and the ladies aren't included under the terms of the charity which pays for it, it was trebles only. Henry Stebbings is responsible for most of the choirboys, being their father, so he drove the minibus full of his own children, and I took the rest in my car. We followed the brown signs that say 'Spend More Time With Your Family at Cliché Theme Park' and arrived in good time. We arranged to meet under the clock, which seemed like a good idea, and let the little chaps go off and enjoy themselves. They enjoyed the Emotional Roller Coaster and the Death-Defying Plunge, thought the Kiss and Tell was soppy, and what they lost on the roundabouts, they won on the swings. And when the clock said, 'At this present moment in time it is 4.00' we rounded them up, and brought them home, tired but happy.

12th August, Ninth Sunday after Trinity
Two nice young ladies came to church, staying here on holiday. They said they were Lesbians, and I remarked that they spoke English very well.

In the afternoon, the annual blessing of walking sticks. I wish people would read the Sunday newsletter. There were at least three crutches brought along. A walking stick is a walking stick and a crutch isn't, and we have to draw the line somewhere. Otherwise where would we be? Blessing wheelchairs, or some such nonsense.

13th August, Monday
A call from Wilkins saying I can take the posters down now, as his curate has come home, safe and well, but with a silly grin on his face. He also has some cuts and bruises, and has probably been in a fight, but Wilkins says he's quite happy, playing with his ball as if nothing had happened.

14th August, Tuesday
Chapter meeting a bit depleted, what with so many being on holiday. And Wilkins' curate having to be led everywhere, because he's wearing a special dog collar to stop him scratching, and he can't see over the rim. But we had a talk on Chasubles – Past,

Present and Future. The future looks very exciting, with chasubles made of Teflon, or Kevlar, so they will be indestructible. Mind you, some of the old ones have lasted pretty well. Apparently a genuine Ribaldi in good condition would be worth a small fortune to a collector. He only made a few for the personal chaplains to the Medici family, and it is said that a mass celebrated in a Ribaldi actually sounds measurably better.

15th August, Wednesday

While I was in the churchyard, contemplating the transience of all things mortal and eating a choc ice, something made me look up, and a spaceship the size of a Strict Baptist Chapel descended, put down three jointy legs, and unfolded a flight of metal steps. Out came a small furry entity with a random assortment of features on what I assumed was its face. It raised a sort of flipper in greeting, and asked me to take it to my leader in a strong Australian accent. I told it to hang on while I phoned the rural dean, and established he was in, which was lucky, because technically, the pubs were still open. The creature was humming the theme from *Neighbours* while it waited, and I pointed out the way to Deeplow, adding that they couldn't miss it,

because it's the only church with a proper steeple for miles, and my leader's name is Barry. 'Barry', it repeated, impressed. Then the alien either bowed, or had cramp, returned to its ship and left as silently as it came, which wasn't silent at all, come to think of it.

16th August, Thursday

Barry the rural dean phoned from Deeplow and asked why I can't handle the simplest thing without consulting him, and why didn't I tell him that yesterday's visitor was going to be a furry entity from a different planet, who thought earth was called Grundy. 'Would you have believed me?' I asked. 'You'd have thought I was a raving nutter, wouldn't you?' 'Oh, rats!' he said. 'What's the matter?' I asked. 'He told me to take him to my leader, and I just sent him to see the archdeacon. Now he's going to think I'm a raving nutter who can't cope.'

17th August, Friday

A child at the communion rail once held up his teddy and I said, 'God bless this bear', with my hand on its head, so I was quite prepared to bless W433LJH's car, coming alongside the people where they are, as the bishop is always saying we have to. The chap formerly known as Micky Speed brought his new car up the drive, and I was there ready in my stole, with a full bucket of water. I said a suitable prayer, and poured the water over the roof of the car. Micky fainted away, landing with a thud on the tarmac, and I thought he'd been slain in the Spirit, so I tipped the last few drops over him to bring him round. I asked him if he was all right and he gasped, 'The sunroof was open!' So it was. Silly me.

18th August, Saturday

Tobias Pigley has died aged 88. He was leaning on his gate, under his cap, as was his wont, greeting complete strangers with a surly nod. He didn't go in for his tea because, as his great-nephew found out, he was dead. Although he never married, he came from a big family – the mammals – and had lots of nieces, nephews and creditors.

I stood a moment before going to bed, looking at the sky, an infinity of spangled blackness. Somewhere there is a planet where the inhabitants are furry entities who know all about the hierarchy of the Anglican Church, on a planet they only know about from watching Australian TV. The thought filled me with a profound sense, but I'm blowed if I know what of.

19th August, Tenth Sunday after Trinity

The baptism of little Jade Goody, who has improved since she was born, and at least you can tell which way she is facing. Baptism went well up to a point, the point at which she wriggled from my grasp. There are times when saying 'Whoops' doesn't seem enough.

20th August, Monday

Great excitement because the archdeacon hasn't been seen since Friday, and missed all his services yesterday. His cleaning lady, Mrs Tombs, who is so insanitary he has to follow her about with a damp cloth, found a cryptic note under the Wallace and Gromit fridge magnet which said 'Razor blades crispbread Jaffa Cakes Odoreaters'.

21st August, Tuesday

I can just feel the whole area spiralling out of control without the steadying hand of the archdeacon. The air is dense with the smoke from piles of burning pine, as vicars take advantage, and remove the pews that the archdeacon has guarded for so long. And as word has got around, I've had to reassure people in the post office and the butcher's that if I were to resign, there would still be some mechanism to replace me. Mrs Smallie asked if that meant their next vicar would be a robot, and I reassured her that as I had no intention of resigning, she needn't worry for a while yet. Wilkins called and said he sent his curate out for the morning paper, and without the threat of being reported to the archdeacon hanging over him, he came back with a copy of *Health and Efficiency* and a box of Maltesers.

22nd August, Wednesday

Keith phoned, and asked me if I'd like to go over this evening for a drink and make up a foursome for a game of Schism, as Canon Hubble is on holiday. This is an exclusive little set I've always felt excluded from, so of course I said I'd go. Hilary asked, 'Will this be every week?' and I said it could be, and she gave me a smile that showed how pleased for me she was. When I got there, Keith pointed over my shoulder and shouted 'Father Ron!' as usual. Drinks turned out to be gin and tonic, or gin without tonic, or tonic without gin, and Keith, Richard Head and Terry Dickson all played Schism as if their lives depended on it, and showed no mercy to me, the raw beginner. Drawing a Huguenot card didn't help, and I'm sure Keith stole my Recant tokens while I wasn't looking, just so he could burn me.

23rd August, Thursday

The Schism box ought to carry a warning that playing the game can give you the symptoms of a hangover. Spent a quiet morning choosing the hymns for next month, and then had to do them all over again because I'd forgotten about Harvest Festival.

In the afternoon, I was called out to Gruntle's farm to see the mysterious circles that have appeared. Ted met me at the gate, and to my surprise, led me indoors and upstairs. On the bedroom carpet were clearly defined patches where the pile had been laid down in a perfectly circular pattern. 'One minute they was there, Vicar,' said Ted, 'and the minute before, they wasn't.' What unknown agency could have caused such a phenomenon? And is there any connection with the archdeacon's disappearance? 'Nobody's been in here,' Ted assured me. 'Only the old dog, and all he does is chase his own tail.'

24th August, Friday
St Bartholomew's Day, but we don't have a special service because the last time it was on a Sunday and I preached about him being skinned, someone was sick. Come to think of it, I think it was me.

Funeral of Tobias Pigley. The church full of people sobbing because they would never see their money again. When I led out to the graveside, everyone followed except the bearers with the coffin, who had followed Henry Dolt to the hearse, and taken the late Tobias to Blicester Crematorium. A frantic phone call prevented a disaster, and everyone went off to the Temporary Sign for the wake, leaving me to do the burial when Henry finally came back. How he grumbled when he realized that he would have to pay for the crematorium and the churchyard, but only be able to charge the family for one.

25th August, Saturday
Two small children in the church-yard looked so solemn I went and spoke to them. They were looking down at a small patch of freshly dug

soil, with two lolly sticks tied together with blue wool to make a little cross. I asked what they were doing, and they told me they had just buried their guinea pig, Harold. 'I'm sorry,' I said. 'When did he die?' One of them looked up, and said, 'Later.' The school holidays are too long.

26th August, Eleventh Sunday after Trinity
A suspected outbreak of cassock weevil. Some insanitary choirboy probably brought it in, and now it's spread. Unconfirmed as yet, but all the telltale signs are there. I can't even call the Council, because it's Sunday.

27th August, Monday
Called the Council to report cassock weevil. The man who answered made teeth-sucking noises, and said he'd be over right away. It is now 11.15pm, and I'm going to bed.

28th August, Tuesday
The man from the Council came in a van with 'Pest Control' on it in huge letters. So much for discretion and confidentiality. He wore shiny white overalls and heavy rubber gloves. He looked at the cassocks and asked, 'Have you had Charismatics?' and I said I hadn't, not knowingly, anyway. And he

said unless he was very much mistaken, this wasn't your ordinary cassock weevil, it was your Toronto Beetle, which usually comes in with Charismatics, and the whole lot will have to be burned. He didn't even handle them with his gloves, but used one of those grabbers-on-a-stick they have in old peoples' homes, and he put them in a bin with a skull and crossbones on the side. He made me sign a paper, and as he drove off, he said the bill would be in the post.

Bible study at Mrs Jellicle's. The great bit in Habakkuk is at the end: 'even though the fig trees have no fruit, and no grapes grow on the vines, even though the olive crop fails and the fields produce no corn, even though the sheep all die and the cattle-stalls are empty, I will still be joyful and glad because the Lord God is my saviour.' I'll remember that the next time I take evensong and there's nobody else there.

29th August, Wednesday

Couldn't sleep again last night wondering who might be Charismatic. Mr McSporran sounds like he's speaking in tongues, but it's just his accent, and Mrs Boyle forgets her glasses, can't read the words and goes 'La-la'. Anybody I catch waving their arms about singing, I'm giving them the bill for the cassocks.

30th August, Thursday
The last tender for the church repairs has come in. The James Brothers' tender is so low they must be planning to skimp on everything they can. They must be the cowboys the archdeacon warned us about. Ike Clanton and Sons could rebuild the church entirely for what they've quoted, and Roy, Rogers and Trigger seem to be within a few hundred of what the architect thought would be the rate. So I had a quick chat with Harry Parry over the phone, and Roy, Rogers and Trigger it is. I wrote to them saying they could start whenever they were ready.

31st August, Friday
That's the thing about August. A quiet month when nothing much happens.

September

September

1st September, Saturday

A fine and sunny day, despite the forecast, and all of Cheeving in a state of festive anticipation. The Village Flower Show is always the occasion for friendly rivalry and actual bloodshed. This year was no exception, with a dispute about

whether you measure the Longest Runner Bean in a straight line from end to end, or along the curve, nearly costing the judge his sanity. I thought my part ended with declaring the show open with a brief prayer, but there was a category for the Potato Most Like the Vicar, which I was asked to judge. It was hard to know whether they were meant to be like all of me, or just my head, but there was a clear winner, which could actually stand in for me for some of the duller acts of worship.

And I won a raffle prize – a free massage and face pack at the New You Centre in Blicester. I gave the voucher to Hilary, and she asked whether I was trying to tell her something, and when I offered to take it back and go myself she said, 'Hah!' derisively.

I wish I'd won the basket of fruit. You know where you are with a basket of fruit. There was an auction afterwards of unclaimed exhibits, and I secured a Picture Made From Pasta Shapes, the Second Heaviest Pumpkin and a Display of Culinary Herbs (not exceeding 12 inches in diameter).

2nd September, Twelfth Sunday after Trinity
What can one say about the Syrian woman that hasn't been said already?

Turning the calendar over in the kitchen before lunch, I remarked as if I'd only just noticed it, 'Do you realize it's my birthday on the 18th?' I wasn't expecting everybody to jump about saying, 'Oh, wow! We must organize a party, and bestow gifts upon you', so I wasn't disappointed.

Only six of us at evensong, so we sat in the choir stalls, and the four that weren't me and Adrian were his family, there to encourage his preaching, and tell him to tell it like it is. I took him aside in the vestry afterwards, and told him firmly there must be no more whooping during the Nunc Dimittis.

3rd September, Monday
A builders' truck arrived full of scaffolding, and parked in the field behind the churchyard. A stout man in a vest peered at a tiny scrap of paper in his huge fist, and up at the tower. Staring at the weather-worn gargoyles around the parapet must have been like looking in his shaving mirror, which he clearly hadn't done for several days. I made 'Hello, can I help you?' noises, and he pointed and

said, 'Is this the church?' I told him it was, and he beckoned to the others in the truck, who began unloading poles, and stacking them under the north wall. I would have loved to have stayed and watched, but it was my day off, and Lego spaceships don't build themselves.

4th September, Tuesday
No sign of the builders, except for a pile of scaffold poles, planks and those clamps that look like medieval tortures. So I went off visiting. When I came back, half the church was covered in scaffolding, but there was still no sign of the builders. Odd. Both boys complained of stomach ache, headache, invisible spots and swollen faces that went down as soon as they opened their mouths. I said they have to go back to school tomorrow anyway, and I wasn't fooled, because I try all these tricks myself, alternate years when there's Clergy Summer School.

5th September, Wednesday
The boys went back to school without too much kicking and screaming, and as soon as I got home, the vicarage seemed strangely quiet.

Midweek service conducted at high volume to compete with the sound of builders erecting scaffolding, and a phone-in quiz on their radio. I thought I was winning until the radio asked, 'Who was Tina Turner's guitar-playing husband?' and Mrs Hooley said, 'Ike', and punched the air.

6th September, Thursday
Hilary said the photocopier wasn't working, but she'd called Mr Hopkins. He came and said the outlet grommets were manky and the shuttle belt was askew. He unmanked the outlet grommets while he drank tea, and said he'd come back with a new shuttle belt. Hilary fetched my diary, and apparently the first day he could come back is Tuesday, while I'm at Chapter. But Hilary will be here to let him in.

7th September, Friday
Heironymus Toofinger-Upping went to a memorial service yesterday simply because it was for someone who had exactly the same name as himself, and he couldn't resist the idea. He was struck by the coincidences in their lives. Both had identical twin brothers who died in bizarre plumbing accidents, both had brothers-in-law who were high court judges, and both had made fortunes breeding rare but desirable strains of canary. He read about it in *The Telegraph*, and knew it wasn't him when he got to the bit about how he was sadly missed by his many friends. 'And the strangest thing was, Vicar,' he said, 'When I told them my name, they all said, "Who?"'

8th September, Saturday
The first match of the new season saw Cheeving Halfpenny resplendent in their new strip, sponsored

by the brewery. So they carried the Busticle's logo proudly on their chests, and gave the Pywicket Eleven a sound thrashing. Then I wished our lads luck, and left them to play football.

9th September, Thirteenth Sunday after Trinity, St Botulus of Thyatira
St Botulus' Day service went off at half-cock because nobody remembered the sausages. So his statue on the rood screen went unadorned. Mrs Macreedy flapped about saying, 'Would a black pudding do?' but I assured her as gently as I could, but with authority, too, that a black pudding would not do.

Despite the fact the service sheets were clearly marked 'Not to be taken away', I had to tackle old Mrs Todger on the churchyard path. There were pearl beads and false teeth everywhere, but I got it back, which is the main thing.

10th September, Monday
A skip has been delivered over the churchyard wall by a vehicle that looked like a prop from *Thunderbirds*. I wrote a couple of letters, and walking down to the post office, I passed three people going the other way carrying mattresses. All very mysterious.

11th September, Tuesday

Clergy chapter. A talk on Pyxes. Canon Hubble immediately said, 'Can't stand the little b****rs! Prancing about in tights, singing silly songs and making the milk sour.' When I got back, the house was apparently empty, but I found Hilary upstairs, asleep and smiling. She said, when I woke her, she hadn't slept at all last night because I was talking in my sleep. I asked her what I was saying, and she said, 'I've no idea – it was all Greek to me.' But I reminded her I don't speak Greek. All a bit of a mystery. The photocopier is going like a greased whippet with its new shuttle belt. They don't make them like they used to.

12th September, Wednesday

Only a week to my birthday, as I pointed out to Hilary and the boys at breakfast. Hilary said, 'Are you going to put it in the Sunday notices?'

An earnest lady from the Wildlife Trust, who appeared to be dressed entirely in recycled Shredded Wheat, called to ask whether the church has any bats, as we're not allowed to do any work which might disturb them. I said we had rocs, giant anteaters and a Thing in the font, but no bats to my knowledge. She insisted on looking for herself, looking for tell-tale signs like droppings, butterfly wings without butterflies, and dead cows without blood. As we passed the yawning gap in the wall, she said, 'Good Lord, is that the builders' crack?' and I'm afraid I couldn't answer for laughing.

13th September, Thursday

I hate it when Mongol hordes, displaced by socio-economic pressures in their homeland, and driven by a desire for conquest and power, come sweeping from the east, burning and pillaging and leaving destruction in their wake. The church stinks of fermented mares' milk for days, and the collection is full of Tugriks.

14th September, Friday

Nahum Fodder, one of my predecessors in this living, has died, aged 99. Legend has it he lied about his age to be ordained, gave out mint humbugs to miners during the General Strike, and once took the crozier from the Bishop of Blicester, straightened out the curl with his bare hands, and gave it back saying, 'There, that's better'. But he is chiefly remembered for appearing in black and white on *What's My Line?* when he wore cassock, alb, chasuble and stole, signed in as Reverend Nahum Fodder, and for his mime, blessed the panel with an extravagant flourish. Gilbert Harding took one look and asked, 'Are you a vicar?' He was never made a Canon. Think about it.

15th September, Saturday

All the flower ladies were in church from first light, decorating for tomorrow's Harvest Festival. There is an ancient tradition here in Cheeving that 13 apples are put on the sill under the window with

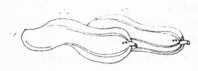

the last supper, and then one is solemnly taken away to symbolize Judas leaving. This little ritual was observed, although Mrs Pryke spoiled it a bit by saying, 'Give us back that apple, you traitor!'

The marrows arrived mid-morning, one or two carried in by their proud producers, but most just crawled in of their own accord, and nestled themselves into the greenery. And then Mrs Todger's husband arrived, hidden behind two giant squeaking sheaves of wheat, which he placed one each side of the chancel arch. All the mice immediately ran out of them, scurrying all over the church, and Mrs Smallie ran out straight after, not to be seen again that day.

16th September, Fourteenth Sunday after Trinity, Harvest Festival.
We sang all the old favourites: 'Come ye thankful people come', 'We plough the fields and scatter', and 'Smite the slugs in thy wrath, O Lord'. No exploding marrows this year, praise be, although with the benefit of hindsight, the ancient local custom of throwing the Harvest Loaf to the choirboys, and giving a penny to whoever gets the biggest bit, would have been better observed outdoors. If looks could kill, Mrs Hopkins would be another Herod.

17th September, Monday
I packed up all the harvest produce and took it over to the old people's bungalows, and left it all with the warden to distribute as she saw fit. At first she seemed really pleased, but as she looked through it, she began to look worried. 'There seems to be a lot of beans,' she said. 'Is that a problem?' I asked. 'It could be,' she said, 'Some of them smoke.'

18th September, Tuesday
My birthday! I looked in the bathroom mirror, and thought I don't look too bad, considering, and a bit of grey lends me a certain dignity. I said to Hilary, 'Don't you think a bit of grey lends me a certain dignity?' and she said, 'Yes, but it ought to be in your hair, not your face.' Hilary gave me a card with a chimpanzee on it, and the Pocket Pulpit that we'd seen in the Van Wipple's catalogue, so now I can preach anywhere. Her parents sent me some new clerical socks, and a sensible card, and the boys gave me some Lego, and offered to build it for me if I'm too busy.

After supper, I went to the Temporary Sign, so that everyone could buy me a drink, and there was nobody there but W433LJH. I wasn't sure whether he'd forgiven me, but I asked, 'Where is everybody, W?' 'TV on the football', he said, obviously trying to remember why he shouldn't be speaking to me at all. But he bought me a drink, and I bought him one, and some time later, he said, 'Something I've always wanted to ask you, Vicar. How can God be three people at the same time?' And then he slid unconscious off his stool before I could tell him.

19th September, Wednesday
As I was crossing the churchyard to do the mid-week service, a loud wolf-whistle made me look up. One of the builders called down, 'Sorry, Padre – force of habit. I thought you was wearing a skirt.'

20th September, Thursday
PCC meeting in the vicarage because the village hall is no more and the church is full of builders. All present except Miss Tredgett who sent her apologies because the wheel had come off her wheelbarrow. The boys came in and tried to sell everyone their homemade coconut ice. But as most coconut ice is pink and white, and this was light grey and dark grey, there were few takers. The meeting itself was mainly about the progress of the works, and how we can raise the rest of the funds to pay for them. It seemed to go on a long time, and I realized it was because they were all warm and comfortable, not like the old village hall or the church. Just as I thought I could send them all home in the cold, somebody tried to bring up a motion, under Any Other Business, that I should say my morning prayers using the *Book of Common Prayer* even when I'm on my own. Maybe we should have meet-

ings in the churchyard. In the rain. Standing on one leg. Anyway, I was congratulated for my efforts in extracting large cheques from people who don't even come to church, and I decided not to admit what the secret is, but simply bask in the adulation. I shall just call on the whole PCC one at a time, and offer to tell everyone all about them.

21st September, Friday

No sign of the builders all day, except Baz the tea boy, who kept coming across to the vicarage asking if I wanted another cup. Eventually I had to give up trying to write a sermon and go out, where the chances of being asked, 'More tea, Vicar?' are slightly lower.

I called on Ted and Todina, and she told me with great glee how much better her arthritis was since she and Ted tied the knot. 'Tied the knot in what?' I asked, dreading what the answer might be.

On the way home, I stopped off at the General Stores for something of a snackish nature to mop up all that tea. Miss Threadgold caught me by the Wotsits and said she thought I'd emigrated because she hadn't seen me for so long. I told her I'd been on holiday, and she said, 'Since May?' and raised a quizzical eyebrow. I said I'd visit her soon, and bring Hilary, too; the eyebrow came down again, and she managed to say, 'I'll look forward to that' without moving her lips.

22nd September, Saturday
I was just putting the finishing
touches to my sermon, like
punctuation, and little
reminders to speak loudly
where the logic is faulty, when
an angel appeared unto me,
and said nothing until I said,
'Yes?' in a friendly way. It
said, 'I'm sure there was
something I had to tell you',
then it said 'No, it's gone.'
And it went.

23rd September, Fifteenth Sunday after Trinity
Not paying the gravity bill turns out to have been a
false economy, as we have been cut off. Hymn
books and congregation all floating about in free-
fall, mingling with kneelers and the builders' dust,
and very disconcerting to see candle flames
pointing downwards. I told Harry Parry to get a
cheque off as
soon as possible,
even if it means
the organ
doesn't get
tuned for
another month.

24th September, Monday

The builders are back. I asked where they were all day Friday, and they all looked at their feet, until one of them said, 'We was called away to a rush job. Sorry.' And then they got stuck into whatever it is they're actually doing with gusto, and Radio Two. After lunch, there was a phone call from the Brigadier, asking whether the builders were there, and I had to shout over the noise of some DJ and his posse, and say yes, they were, and he said, 'Ask them when they're coming to finish my wall – they made a start Friday and I haven't seen them since, and the goats are coming in.'

25th September, Tuesday

Bible study group looked at Zephaniah. Lots of doom and punishment, which seemed to suit some people, who think God is altogether too soft these days. And when it came to the bit about whole nations being wiped out, the Colonel said, 'I could write him a list.'

26th September, Wednesday, St Giles

Not *the* St Giles, but St Giles the Farmer, the patron saint of sufferers. I keep saying we should get the statue of him on the rood screen restored, but nobody knows what it should look like, although everybody thinks they know. He was a martyr, of course, but as Mrs Drew says, aren't we all?

Gravity back on, and everything is back as it

was. Even the dust from the building work has settled back exactly where it was, and Mrs Hopkins assures me that if I think she's cleaning up after them by herself, I'm very much mistaken. I assured her we'd have a working party, and she snorted, 'And I suppose *they'll* want coffee.'

27th September, Thursday

Dennis Elbeau says if the organ isn't tuned soon, it won't matter who plays it, as all the notes will sound the same. When I suggested maybe this is the time to replace it with the best electronic organ we can afford, actual steam came out of his ears, and his face turned the colour of a victoria plum. And when I tried to calm him down by saying the modern ones have built in drums and bass, he turned as pale as an Easter lily. Don't say I can't write descriptively.

28th September, Friday

The archdeacon is back! He claims to have spent the last month with the furry entities on a distant planet very different from our own, where the sky is pink, there is only one sex, and people smile as they share the Peace. Mrs Tombs (who is Mrs Hopkins' sister – it seems that cleaning is a family tradition) says she asked him about the cryptic note on the fridge, and apparently he clapped his hand to his forehead in horror, saying, 'I knew there was something I'd forgotten – razor blades!' The bishop appears to think it's all down to stress.

29th September, Saturday
Harry Parry has done some calculations, and visited the music shops in Blicester, and it seems the best electronic organ we could afford is 14 inches wide. And, he added gloomily, the batteries are extra.

30th September, Sixteenth Sunday after Trinity
Dennis is obviously feeling threatened, as he pulled out all the stops for the processional, with the result that mice were actually seen hovering in the air columns over some of the pipes. Then there was a near tragedy as Miss Tredgett, egged on by her sister, Miss Tredgett, was playing chicken across the aisle, and the procession didn't stop. The crucifer, Barry, is a growing lad, as the broken light fittings testify, and she was badly trampled by him, two acolytes with candles, the whole choir, and Adrian the Reader.

October

1st October, Monday

A titanic battle between
Good and Evil took
place in the vicarage
kitchen. Our man
appeared naked and

rosy cheeked, whichever way he was facing, except
you aren't supposed to notice that, what with him
being a cherub. He claimed to have posed for
Poussin once, and fielded a shiny new conker,
whereas Evil, I am convinced, had baked his, or
pickled it in vinegar, or whatever it is the unscrupu-
lous do these days. They traded blows evenly for
several minutes, as the tension rose, but finally Evil
swung his conker and missed, and the string wound
around his neck. Good claimed the victory, while
Evil stamped his little hooves furiously, until he dis-
integrated in a burst of orange flame. Hilary had
the presence of mind to drop a wet tea towel on the
place, while Good flew off, chanting 'Ea-sy, ea-sy!',
and thanked us for the Bovril.

2nd October, Tuesday

There I was, just outside the churchyard, picking
up walnuts, when up comes old Mr Turvey shaking
his stick at me. 'You can't have them!' he ranted,
'They ain't glebe nuts!' 'No,' I said, quick as a flash,
'they're walnuts. And the tree is in the churchyard.'
'But the nuts are on the verge,' said Mr Turvey, as
if that settled the matter. I suggested that if he

wanted some walnuts he could help himself, just like me, but he said that wasn't the point, and tried to wrestle my carrier bag from me, whacking my shins with his cane.

3rd October, Wednesday
It occurred to me that the verge outside the church-yard might actually be church land, too. So I phoned Church House and asked to speak to the diocesan archivist. A familiar throaty voice asked 'When do you want the fire?' I asked to be put back to the switchboard. She said, 'Sorry, I thought you said arsonist', which is wearing a bit thin now, don't you think?

4th October, Thursday
The whole church is now swathed in polythene sheets like a Cristo installation, and the noise of it flapping in the wind can be heard all over the village. For the time being, even though the weather vane from the church tower is away being repaired and regilded, I have excused the sidesmen of their duty of taking turns standing on the tower, pointing into the wind.

The weather forecast is for storms, high winds, and animated arrows the size of Cornwall all over the place. When I put the cat out, it blew back in.

5th October, Friday
Writing by candlelight as the power has been off since 7 o'clock this evening. Wind howling in the

trees, and Hilary came back from her banjo lesson with her umbrella inside out and both earrings on her leeward ear. Dustbin lids were rolling down the street like, well, like dustbin lids, and the cat was sucked up the chimney.

6th October, Saturday
During last night's storm, the church was actually blown a foot and a half to the northeast. People who think it's a long haul up the churchyard path will find it's even longer now. Power still off, so we had tuna sandwiches for supper, and the boys think it's a great treat being allowed to have cereal three times a day, but they're having computer game withdrawal symptoms. They really think that Ice Cool Coyote will miss them.

7th October, Seventeenth Sunday after Trinity
Woken up in the small hours by all the lights coming on, plus the TV, radio, fridge and telephone answering machine. Stumbled about turning everything off, and went back to bed, but felt a bit duntish for the rest of the day.

Because it's the nearest Sunday to St Francis' Day, we had the annual Blessing of Pets.

Despite a strict 'No Slugs' rule, several turned up, all except one in jars. We sang 'All things bright and beautiful', 'Who put the colours in the rainbow' and 'Now thank we all our dog', with words by yours truly. Quite a lot of the animals joined in. It's no bad thing that Damian isn't able to come onto consecrated ground, because it's rumoured he has a pet cockatrice, and heaven only knows what would happen if anyone tried to bless it.

Mrs Hopkins says forget about the new Hoover bag, she now needs a new Hoover, which is fair enough. Maybe the goat wasn't such a good idea after all.

8th October, Monday
A strange smell in the church when I went to unlock. It wasn't Alice the anteater, and it wasn't the goat. It had a distinct tang of hyena. What else did I miss yesterday?

9th October, Tuesday
A ring-tailed lemur, that's what. The builders have been giving it cake. If nobody comes for it before next weekend, I shall mention it in the Sunday notice sheet. I wish people wouldn't use the Pets Service to dispose of their unwanted animals. No wonder we have a Thing in the font.

Chapter meeting. Talk on Celibacy. 'Don't worry,' he quipped, 'You can't catch it off your parents.' I'm more concerned I seem to be catching it off my wife. I can't remember the last time I wasn't celibate. Maybe the boys are giving Hilary such a bad time she thinks they're not an experiment she wants to repeat.

10th October, Wednesday
A letter arrived from the archdeacon. My annual ministry review is due, which amounts to an interview with that dignitary. I guess by the 26th he'll be back on the same planet as the rest of us.

11th October, Thursday
I spent the morning visiting the elderly and crochety, the bereaved, the sick, the lonely, the unhappy, and the spiritually unfulfilled. And all by just dropping in on Mrs Goodenough. What makes me want to laugh is that when she opened the door and I asked how she was, she said, 'Mustn't grumble', and then did, for 45 minutes without stopping.

12th October, Friday
No jobs in *Church Times* unless I want to be chaplain of a girls' school, with responsibility for the pastoral care of 150 young ladies up to the age of 18. It's not that I can't see myself doing it, but I can't imagine for one moment Hilary *letting* me do it.

13th October, Saturday

Hilary's birthday, and after last year's fiasco, I didn't dare forget. There are still beans on the ceiling. The boys gave her some Lego, and I bought her some of her favourite perfume, *Jezebel*. In the evening, I bribed Shirley Heavily to sit with the boys, warned them they were to give her no non-

sense, and warned her not to put up with any. I took Hilary to El Andamnacion, the Spanish restaurant in Blicester. Eager to show off my Spanish, I ordered with great confidence, and the waiter brought me a pair of wellingtons and a street map of Carlisle. Hilary smiled tolerantly, spoke to the waiter, and he brought us some food.

14th October, Eighteenth Sunday after Trinity

Mr Heavily called to say Shirley wouldn't be in church because she was in a state of nervous exhaustion after babysitting for the boys last night, and whatever I paid her it wasn't enough.

The Scouts presented their old Scoutmaster, Charles Goodturn, to be laid up in the church until he turns to dust, alongside the old British Legion banner. A very moving ceremony, and there were a few tears, but the new Scoutmaster seems to be a good egg, resplendent in brown corduroy, with a

smart black leather woggle. One of the boys addres-
sed him as Führer. He smiled at me, and muttered,
'Just my little joke, Vicar.'

I asked the boys what they had done to Shirley,
and they both said 'Nothing' so promptly my sus-
picions were aroused.

15th October, Monday
Carlisle has a station called Citadel, and a street
called English Damside. How weird is that? Hilary
caught me poring over the map, and said, 'You
didn't bring that home, did you?' I assured her that
as I'd paid for it, I certainly did.

16th October, Tuesday
I found Baz, the builders' tea boy, sitting in the
garage reading the *Dandy,* and berated him for
a lazy young scapegrace. But he said Big Dave
Trigger had sent him off for a Long Weight, and far
from being fooled by this ageing prank, he knew a
good thing when he saw it.
It reminded me of my own
youth, when I was once
sent off for 12 Hail
Marys, and given
a bucket.
If the amounts
of cement being
mixed are any
indication, work

on the church is coming on well. And I can see how young Baz would prefer reading his comic to being thrust into the cement mixer, which was the last practical joke played on him.

17th October, Wednesday

There is an old myth that clergymen use strips cut from washing-up liquid bottles when they run out of dog collars. It can't be true because I couldn't find any collars this morning because the washing machine ate the last one, and it was midweek service and everything, and the bottle was nearly empty anyway. So I had to do the service without moving my head because my jugular vein was exposed to the razor-sharp edge, plus the Colonel took me aside afterwards and whispered, 'I say, Vicar – you're not *really* a Fairy, are you?'

18th October, Thursday

Clergy quiet day with the Little Brothers of St Kevin at Lower Albotes. And it took some finding, being on that part of the map which is mostly white with 'Here be dragons' on it. After the noise of the builders for what seems more than just six weeks, I thought a bit of quiet would do me good. Brother Bartholomew, who is the biggest Little Brother I've ever seen, spoke on The Value of Silence for an hour, until his voice gave out. But it made a change not to have to worry about anything at all for a whole day, except why it is monks seem to eat nothing but macaroni cheese. And one of the monks looked shocked, and said it's very bad form to refer to it. They always call it The Scottish Pasta.

Hilary told me Terry had been to fix the photocopier. I wasn't aware of problems, but apparently there was ink on the nipples and the bed shaft was bent.

19th October, Friday
I looked up St Ipend in the *Dictionary of Saints* and he seems not to exist. I think the cartoonist in *Church Times* might have made him up. How childish. Another of those days when there is nothing in the diary, so I just spent it visiting people and sharing the Good News. I even managed to find the Jehovah's Witnesses in, told them how they could have eternal life, and sold them a copy of the church magazine.

20th October, Saturday
Hilary has a nasty cold, so I cooked lunch for her and the boys. They all looked at it and asked what it was, and was it something foreign. And I said no, fish fingers are British. The boys said, 'Fish fingers are yellow', and I said, 'Not always.'

Wrote a cracker of a sermon about how you don't have to go along with the crowd, you can resist. Just like a sailing boat, you can tack against the

.wind, and it might be harder work than just drifting with the wind and the current, but you get where you're going. I might have laid on the sailing metaphor a bit thick, but I read it over to Hilary and she said if she feels as groggy as she does tonight she won't be in church tomorrow anyway.

21st October, Nineteenth Sunday after Trinity

Just going down the road to get a paper, I saw there were postcards in the village phone box advertising the services of women of a certain profession. Disgusting. If I want a taxi I shall expect a man to drive it. Then trying to find a Sunday paper that wasn't full of salacious tittle-tattle and provocative pictures was nearly impossible. So I abandoned the sailing sermon at the last minute and preached off the cuff about the way sex seems to be everywhere these days, and you can't pick up a magazine, or turn on the TV without sex in some form looming out at you. It seemed to go down all right, if the number of dropped jaws was anything to go by. Hilary feeling better.

22nd October, Monday

Down at the post office, old Len winked at me and said to Hilary, 'That were a grand sermon Vicar preached yesterday – I didn't know he knew so much about it', and she said, 'He doesn't – he's only done it once. He was sick and his hat blew off.'

23rd October, Tuesday
The Bible study group looked at Haggai, whose prophecies all come timed and dated. It doesn't say, but he probably worked for the post office. We all agreed that Haggai would have asked for the angel's ID, and given him a receipt when he'd delivered his message.

24th October, Wednesday
Straight after the midweek service, I packed up sandwiches and a flask of coffee, and set off for Blicester hospital to visit the sick. The nurse at Joseph Stalin said I couldn't see Mrs Boyle because visiting wasn't until 3 o'clock. I smiled and pointed to my dog collar, and she said, 'Not even if you're the chief rabbi – come back at three.' So I went off to see Old Ted, who was glowing radiantly with jaundice, lighting up Bokassa Ward like a little ray of sunshine. He opened one terrible eye, saw my dog collar looming over his bed, and said, 'I'm not that bloody ill.'

25th October, Thursday
I was in the study, photocopying the hymn lists for November, because it was choir practice tonight, when Hilary came in, and asked if the machine was behaving itself. I assured her it was, and gave it a friendly pat. To my surprise, she scowled at it, and gave it a kick in the trolley. Very odd.

On the grounds that an evening in the pub is

worth a week of pastoral visiting, plus I fancied a pint of Busticle's, I took myself off to the Temporary Sign, where I tried to start a discussion on the issue of double predestination. I would have been interested to hear what ordinary people's views on the subject were, but they seemed more interested in what's going on in some place called Albert Square, wherever that is.

26th October, Friday
Over to Tannersworth to see the archdeacon for my regular pep talk and ministry review. Time on an alien world seems not to have had any lasting ill effect, as I doubt if he would have known who I was anyway, without my name in his diary. But he'd remembered Hilary's name, and the boys', and asked how they were, and then asked about my ministry. I was itching to ask him how things were on the other side of the galaxy, or wherever he spent his little holiday, but the opportunity never arose. He asked me how many funerals I'd done this year, and I told him, and he looked as if it wasn't enough, as if there was anything I could do about it. And then he said 'I'm concerned about the development of your ministry', which is archdeacon speak for 'I don't think we're working you hard enough.'

27th October, Saturday
The boys decided they wanted to join the Cheeving junior football team, attracted by the vast sums of

money the top players get when they're grown up, often the price of a pint. So we reported for duty at the playing field, where I joined all the other fathers on the touchline, and tried to blend in by digging my hands in my pockets and shouting 'Get stuck into him!' whenever the occasion seemed to demand it. But we were there less than half an hour because the boys absolutely refused to be more than three feet away from each other at any time. Eventually the coach suggested they try a sport more suited to their obvious talents, like three-legged racing.

Late in the evening, I went around the vicarage putting all the clocks back, because I'd remembered, and then Hilary told me she'd already done it, so I went round putting them all forward again.

28th October, Last Sunday after Trinity
Irate phone call from the Brigadier asking why the church was locked, and he'd wasted a journey. I pointed out that the clocks have gone back, and he must have forgotten and he said, 'Gone back? Gone back where?' and put the phone down before I could explain.

Barry Tripp's mobile phone went off during the service, and he answered it while the rest of us were saying the Prayer for Fewer Sprouts, which was a bit disturbing. As we were shaking hands afterwards, he patted his top pocket and said, 'What did we do before they were invented?' I said, 'I guess we just shouted, "Yo, Craig, see you in the pub at half-past 12"'

29th October, Monday

Ted has discharged himself from hospital, despite being a very odd colour still. I joked that he ought to be green until Advent, and then he could be purple, and he didn't have the faintest idea what I was talking about.

Hilary made an alarming discovery mucking out the boys' room. A large jar with a label saying 'snails'. The lid was off and it was empty.

30th October, Tuesday

Baz the tea boy was measuring scaffold-boards, adding figures up in the margin of his *Whizzer and Chips*, and then trying to measure himself with the same metal tape, and nearly cutting himself in two. I could stand it no longer, and asked what he was up to. He pointed to the planks, and said, 'They all say I'm as thick as them, but I'm not.' I said no, he wasn't, and he shouldn't listen to what they say. He smiled. 'That's right,' he said, holding out his spread fingers, 'I'm that much thicker!'

31st October, Wednesday

There are three sorts of Hallowe'en callers and it's essential to know the difference. The ones who think a Hershey Bar, whatever that may be, is a treat have only heard about it off American sitcoms and can be sent away safely. The hard cases like little Austin must be bought off because having your lock filled with cream cheese is the very least they will do. The ones that leave actual smoking hoof prints can be offered a Mars bar if you want to see it melt, but I keep a Super Soaker filled with holy water, and ask them if they feel lucky. Little Austin called just after *Coronation Street*. I pretended to be frightened, admired his horns, and gave him a Fun Size Twix. He went off quite happily, leaving a trail of smoking hoof prints.

November

1st November, Thursday

PCC meeting in church, in view of the fact there is no village hall, thanks to the Bloats and the Orrells. The promise is that a new one will rise like a phoenix from the ashes of the old, but the parish council seem to be sitting there waiting for it to happen, rather than actually doing anything about it. All present except Henry Stebbings who sent his apologies because the nit shampoo has to be left on overnight. The main item on the agenda was the bazaar. I suggested we have the bazaar in the church, and everyone said, 'Can we do that, Vicar?' and I said we could. It will be a squeeze, and we'll have to do some heavy duty clearing up afterwards, but it's possible. Mrs Smallie raised the question 'Will God mind?' and I said she could leave that to me, I'll explain the circumstances and I'm sure he'll understand.

I reminded everyone that Christmas this year is on 25 December, and Mrs Thomas asked why does it always have to come at the busiest time of the year?

2nd November, Friday

The man came to look at the church and advise us about the heating, which is a service the electricity company provides free. He looked around at our convectors, and the little radiant heater in the vestry, and the under-the-seat job that has slightly warmed generations of organists' bottoms. He poked his calculator, sucked his front teeth, and suggested that the best way to heat St Gargoyle's would be a small fast-breeder nuclear reactor, which would have the added advantage that any radioactive waste would be weapons grade, and would provide an extra source of income to help pay our diocesan share, or at least get the fire extinguishers serviced.

3rd November, Saturday
All those people who can't wait until the 5th to have their bonfires and fireworks had their bonfires and fireworks. The sky was lurid with colour, and the noises sent the cat hysterical. It could be worse. Wilkins says his curate dives into his basket at the first hint of a bang, and doesn't come out until daylight. Still, if I hadn't left writing my sermon until the last minute, I'd have gone outside to watch. A sermon for All Saints' Day takes some writing, because you don't want to leave any out. Our own rood screen in the church seems fairly comprehensive, but some of the more obscure Cornish saints are missing, and one or two sixteenth-century Protestant martyrs, so I feel the need to redress the omissions in my preaching. And what I know about St Pirran you could write on the back of a stamp.

November

4th November, All Saints' Sunday

Hilary says she hasn't sent my cassock to the cleaners, nor has she tried washing it, on the grounds that it hasn't been washed or cleaned ever, and she thought I liked it that way. So where is it? I can't have left it anywhere, because if I do house communions, it's easier to take the cassock-alb, despite old Mrs Mortimer saying it makes me look like the Grand Dragon of the Ku Klux Klan, and makes her glad she's white.

We had our traditional evening service where we invite people to light a candle, and place it on the altar in memory of a loved one. Note for next year: Don't!

5th November, Monday

I was planning to do nothing at all today, as it was supposed to be my day off, but Mrs General at the Stores told me the Bloats have a new baby, so I took myself to Ferret's Bottom, picking my way through the abandoned fridges, to see if I could interest them in a block booking at the font. A huge bonfire was being dismantled by the fire brigade as it was taller than the houses it was only a few feet away from, and being built up again just as fast on the other side of the road by the local truants, most of whom were Shane Bloat's children.

The new baby is delightful. There are two sorts of babies: worried babies and surprised babies. This is a surprised baby. I asked Mrs Bloat what she would call him, and she counted off the letters of the alphabet on her fingers until she got to I. 'Something beginning with I', she said.

Fortunately it was a dry day, because there was no Plan B for the bonfire this year, what with the village hall being a ruin, and the parish council still wrangling over whether to apply for Lottery money. The boys came back from the party at the sportsfield covered in grime, full of hot dogs, a little singed around the edges, but happy. The guy, they reported, had been a great success, dressed as a wizard in a long black robe.

6th November, Tuesday
Called on the Brigadier to ask him to lay the wreath on Sunday. He said he'd be delighted, called me Dear Boy, and then said, 'When I was in Africa . . .' so I faked my own death to get away.

7th November, Wednesday
Off to Cassocks R Us, having given up hope of ever seeing my old cassock again. Just one of life's little

mysteries. I'm sure all the shop assistants in clerical outfitters are failed clergy, especially the unctuous chap who sidled up to me and asked how he could help Sir. I said I needed a new cassock, and he straightened himself up and asked, 'Is Sir being . . . elevated?' I hadn't a clue what he was talking about, until he said, 'Will Sir be wanting . . . purple?' I told him no, black would be fine, and he deflated visibly, and then started asking me about single-breasted, double-breasted, how many buttons I wanted and which side did I dress. And he insisted on measuring my inside leg, 'Just to be on the safe side, Sir.'

In another part of the shop, a clergyman was trying on a cassock and practising golf swings in it, which gives you food for thought. Out of the confusion I emerged with a new cassock, all stiff, and not shiny like the old one, but I expect I'll get used to it. As soon as I got home, I put it on to show Hilary and the boys. 'How do I look?' I asked, giving them a twirl. 'Like the Guy on Monday,' said the boys. What funny little chaps they are.

8th November, Thursday
Mrs General tapped on the shop window as I went past, so I went in. 'It's your bazaar next week, isn't it?' she said. 'I'll give you something for the raffle.' And she did. It was a Cornish pasty.

According to Hilary, the photocopier counter is irregular, and Terry says it will need a new trammelling chute. Soon it will be like the broom that had three new heads and a new handle. But Hilary says Terry will be along to fix it next Tuesday while I'm at Chapter. Terry?

9th November, Friday
Where does all the jam come from? People have been bringing jam for the bazaar, and it's piling up in the kitchen, and I suspect it's the same jam that was sold at the summer fête coming back to haunt us. In fact, I think it's the same jam we sold at last year's bazaar, and people buy jam to eat from the General Store, and jam to recirculate at the fête and bazaar.

10th November, Saturday
Despite our saying the bazaar isn't a jumble sale, still people bring us stuff they're ashamed to leave out for the dustmen, and the garage is filling with other people's rubbish. Nobody ever gives us a cast-off Van Gogh, or an Aston Martin they don't want any more. And that little egg with the coloured glass is a waste of space. Mrs Gross said it might be a Fabergé, but it doesn't smell of any-

thing, and in any case, who's going to buy an Easter egg in November?

11th November, Remembrance Sunday

Cadets, Scouts, Guides, Cubs, Brownies, Tony the policeman and the butcher in his apron, which he insists is a uniform, all paraded in fine style at the War Memorial. The Brigadier laid the wreath when he was pointed in the right direction, and then all into church to sing 'O valiant hearts' and 'I vow to thee my country'. Church full – the only time it ever is apart from Christmas. And the collection goes to the British Legion. Damn, damn, damn!

12th November, Monday

The scaffolding is down, the polythene sheets are off, and the last skip has been swung on to the back of the lorry. Roy, Rogers, and Big Dave Trigger have restored the church, and it doesn't look any different. So the crack in the south wall has been healed up, and the roof doesn't leak and nobody has been squashed by a falling gargoyle since the late Mr Mortimer, but if anybody looks at the bill and asks where the money has gone, I'll be hard put to answer them. I could do with a new pair of shoes, but I daren't buy any in case someone thinks I've been embezzling the funds. It was bad enough trying to explain the new cassock.

13th November, Tuesday
Chapter meeting. Talk on Buddhist Worship, by Logsap Lumpa, who has one of those haircuts that look like chemotherapy and doesn't wear anything that comes from an animal. There's something to be said for being Church of England, where you can go bald in your own time, wear pork scratchings and eat Hush Puppies. Home to find Hilary singing happily, arranging flowers in a vase.

14th November, Wednesday
As I was leaving the church after the midweek service, I thought I heard an angel speaking unto me. I looked up, and there was Baz, the builders' tea boy, calling down plaintively from the top of the tower. I retraced my steps, climbed the tower staircase, shinned up the aluminium ladder, crawled across the bell frame, up the wooden steps, and unbolted the trapdoor. Apparently, when the work was done and the scaffolding came down, he was just abandoned up there, and had been there ever since. I was going to ask what he had been living on, but he had feathers stuck to his unshaved chin, so I thought better of it.

15th November, Thursday
Hilary found a Cornish pasty in the fridge, and was about to throw it away, but I told her it

was a raffle prize for Saturday. 'Have you seen the sell-by date?' I told her yes, it was the end of November. 'Not the month,' said Hilary, 'I meant the year.'

In the afternoon, I took myself down to the old people's bungalows. Most of the residents have been in Cheeving all their lives, and it's good they don't have to leave now. Old Ted, who is still a bit off colour, told me he could remember when the men from Ferret's Bottom used to come into Cheeving Halfpenny on a Saturday night specifically to fight each other. The Temporary Sign had been called something else then, but he couldn't remember what. He recounted a blood-curdling story about a pitched battle that resulted in the Bloats knocking out all the Orrells and piling them up outside the butcher's in a heap. I said, 'That must have been Shane Bloat and Jason Orrell's grandfathers.' Ted looked at me as if I was mad, and said, 'No, it was them two. This were last week.'

16th November, Friday

Everything moveable has been moved out of the way, and the church is ready for the bazaar. I even stuck a piece of plaster over the date on Sir Rodney de Cheeving's tomb, so we can charge people to guess it. By promising they could have a proper Flower Festival next year, I managed to persuade the flower ladies to leave the window sills clear for homemade cakes, soft toys, and those little boxes with seashells glued all over them that always turn up at bazaars. Mrs Hopkins saw all the jam coming in and muttered, 'It will all end in tears, mark my words.' Mrs Jellicle brought lots of mince pies, which are either a bit early or very late. And Mrs Tilley, who is fairly new to the parish asked, 'Would it be sacrilegious to use the font as a bran tub?' And I said, no, not sacrilegious, just very, very unwise.

17th November, Saturday
Just finished putting the church to rights and ready for tomorrow. The bazaar was a tremendous success. The boys stayed out of the way, playing in the churchyard with their friends. People who haven't been in the church since they were babies and might not have come again outside a box were there, parting with their money. Cakes sold like hot cakes, and I even heard that people were buying those little boxes with sea shells glued all over them. The Thing in the font never stirred, probably because we kept the lid on, and I must tell Henry Stebbings that hoop-la with the saints on the rood screen was a touch of genius. All that, and I won a raffle prize, too. It was a Cornish pasty.

18th November, Second Sunday before Advent
The new cassock isn't like the old one. I can't remember whether the old one was stiff and uncomfortable when it was new, but this one is

tight under the arms, so it's just as well I don't go in for evangelical arm-waving. Or golf, come to think of it. And when I take it off, I don't have to hang it up. It stands.

19th November, Monday
The boys came down to breakfast looking very pleased with themselves, and presented me with £7.85, all in small change. 'For the bazaar,' they said. 'Sorry it's late, but we had to lean on some of our clients.' I asked them where they had got the money, and they said snail racing in the church-yard during the bazaar.

They charged own-ers an entry fee, and had a book, too. I was very touched. 'It's very good of you,' I said, 'to give all your money to the church.' They said, 'That's not all of it – just 10 per cent.'

20th November, Tuesday
Applications are already coming in from couples who want to get married next year. Somebody I've never heard of rang this morning, saying he has to book so far ahead because the hotel where he wants his reception is much in demand. My stock response to the question 'Can you marry us on the first Saturday in August next year?' is 'No, I've got a funeral booked for that day.' It has never raised a laugh yet.

21st November, Wednesday

Fog and white frost. It's days like this that make me feel I'm called to minister to the poor benighted heathen in the tropics. A South Sea Island would be nice, if *Mutiny on the Bounty* is anything to go by. Vicar of Tahiti has a nice sound to it. It would be different to visit parishioners who weren't wearing thick tweeds, and be offered coconut milk instead of tea. I know it would be a tough job, with no phone, and no photocopier always going wrong, but somebody has to do it. I wish the Lord would be a bit more clear about it.

22nd November, Thursday

It was a cold evening, so Adrian the Reader and I shared a bottle of something Australian while Hilary was out at her welding class. He wants to know why he isn't allowed to bless people. I wanted to say he can bless who he likes, but that isn't what the Church says. Officially, as I understand it, he can say the blessing, but people aren't actually blessed because God doesn't take any notice of Readers. Then he asked, 'What about a diaconal blessing?' but by that time the second bottle was nearly empty, so I said a diaconal blessing is when you make the sign of the cross like an X. It was funnier when I said it, honestly.

23rd November, Friday
There must be a sort of six-hour flu going around. I woke up with a bad headache and a sore throat, and thought I was being punished for giving my cod liver oil to the cat. I phoned Adrian to tell him, so he would be ready to do services on Sunday if I was no better by then. But he said he'd got it too, but in any case, by the time I'd had coffee and breakfast, I felt a lot better. And Hilary was quite unsympathetic, saying it wasn't flu, but Woogulooga Creek.

I crept out after lunch to do some visiting, and there's nothing like being with people who are actually ill to make you feel a whole lot better.

24th November, Saturday
As everything was ready for tomorrow (sermon written, notice sheet photocopied, wafers counted and new candles on the altar), I went off to the field to watch Cheeving Halfpenny play Tannersworth at football. And who should be there but the archdeacon, supporting the away side. We had a short theological discussion on whether God was more likely to listen to his prayers for his team than mine, what with him being an archdeacon and every-

thing, but we came to the conclusion that God doesn't mind who wins, as long as it's a good, clean, sporting competition. In which case, he was very disappointed. And so, incidentally, was the archdeacon.

25th November, Sunday before Advent, Christ the King
A special service of thanksgiving for the completion of the restoration work. All those who contributed to the fund were invited to come and admire the church looking its best, and ready to face the next hundred years. A very happy occasion, marred only by one small mishap. We always admire Jennifer the Sunday school teacher because she really makes the Bible come alive for the little  ones. But today it ate little Archie Stebbings before Jennifer knew what was happening. And we knew nothing about it until much later, as the congregation gave us so many curtain calls, we nearly missed lunch.

26th November, Monday
Day off. Too wet and windy to go out, so I decided to clear out the loft. All right, Hilary put it to me that clearing out the loft would be a Really Good Idea, with that steely look in her eyes that even

works on the boys, sometimes. Behind the water tank I found a box of church magazines, as far as I could tell, a complete set dating back to the 1940s when it was just one sheet folded because there was a war on. Otherwise nothing seems to have changed, even down to Mrs Hopkins being thanked for cleaning the church. And there were jokes, too. The one about any ladies wishing to become young mothers should see the vicar in the vestry after the service appears to be 60 years old. And I thought I'd made it up.

27th November, Tuesday

A foul night, and the Bible study group was a bit depleted. But we all enjoyed Zechariah, who had visions like conjuring tricks. He was shown a basket, which was opened to reveal a woman (in my Bible there's a picture, and she looks quite tasty. But she represents sin, apparently.) Then the lid was closed and the basket was flown off to Babylon. 'So,' I said at the end, 'What lessons can we learn from Zechariah?' and the Colonel said, 'Find out what he's drinking and order a pint.'

Home to find Hilary in her dressing-gown, with Terry Hopkins, drinking a glass of wine. Apparently, Hilary was just about to have a bath when he called on his way home to make sure the photocopier was behaving itself, which was very considerate of him, and Hilary was right to offer him a drink.

28th November, Wednesday
Hilary was studying her Bible before breakfast. I looked over her shoulder, and she was reading Zechariah. 'I thought Zechariah was much longer than that', she said.

29th November, Thursday
Doing the hymn list for next month was an absolute doddle. When I'd done, I took them round to Dennis Elbeau so he could check that no rogue tunes had crept in that the congregation wouldn't know. Then he said, 'I was going to ask you, Vicar,' and went all conspiratorial. 'I've written a carol,' he blurted out at last, blushing to his roots. 'I wonder if we might sing it this year.' 'Let's hear it', I said. He sat down at the piano, and sang, 'While shepherds once in David's city, Heard the frosty wind make moan, Angels from the realms of glory, Came upon the midnight clear.' The tune was vaguely familiar. I said I'd think about it.

30th November, Wednesday
Strolling along the corniche in the early hours after a good night at the casino, my bow tie undone and my wallet full of cash, I was accosted by a beautiful redhead in an evening dress. 'Help me,' she cried, urgently, 'They'll kill me if they catch me.' So I hurried her into my Porsche, and set off, tyres squealing, with a black Jag in hot pursuit, taking the hairpin bends with ease, her long blonde hair

blowing behind her. Their bullets whistled past us, until we shook off our pursuers, somewhere near Nice, and she turned to me, her long black hair framing her perfect features, and said, 'How can I ever thank you?' I raised a suggestive eyebrow, woke up, and had a really dull day.

December

December

1st December, Saturday

I have been nominated Preacher of the Year! The winner is announced at a lunch on the 13th. I feel proud, and yet humble. I showed the invitation to Hilary, so she could start thinking about what to wear, but she seemed unimpressed by the whole business. Finally, she gave me the letter back and said, 'Just look who the award is from!' I did. The Insomnia Society. The first door in my Advent calendar had a tennis racket in it.

2nd December, Advent Sunday

What with Epiphany and Candlemas, why don't I learn? The Advent wreath ought to have an X certificate. Certainly asking little Robin Pules to light a red candle, and putting a lighted taper in his hands was like dropping a fox in a chicken coop. But we've got evacuation down to a fine art.
Nothing like the threat of cremation for making the lame leap.

3rd December, Monday

Opened the third door in my Advent calendar and there was a traffic cone in it. After yesterday's spider, maybe I shouldn't have been surprised. The boys have taken to leaving catalogues lying around with particular items circled in felt tip. I have no idea what most of these things are.

Hilary has been busy typing a newsletter to go in our Christmas cards, telling all our friends what has been happening in the last year. I don't know how she can think of anything to write, it's been such a quiet year.

4th December, Tuesday

The MacWhirters' toaster is possessed by an evil spirit. Brown bread actually comes out white, and white bread comes out transparent. I laid hands on it and commanded the spirit to come out. It refused,

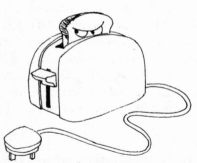

and the toaster started to smoke, even though it wasn't plugged in. I rang Canon Hardcastle, the diocesan exorcist, who once forced a whole troop of small cast-out demons to clear his churchyard with their teeth, and he said not to try anything with holy water, and he'd be right over. Within the hour, he was there, and I asked about the holy water, and he explained that in cases like this, it can actually antagonize the evil entity, plus it's likely to blow the fuses.

The job was done in minutes, and Mrs MacWhirter thanked us, apologized that she couldn't offer us tea, and said she'd been planning a new kitchen anyway, although maybe not before Christmas.

5th December, Wednesday
The WI held their annual carol service in church, with mulled wine and mince pies afterwards. Good to hear all the old favourites again.

6th December, Thursday
Opened the sixth door on my Advent calendar. A football boot. The Mothers' Union held their annual carol service in church, with mulled wine and mince pies afterwards. Good to hear all the old favourites again. As most of the Mothers' Union are also members of the WI, and vice versa, it was good to see all the old favourites again as well.

7th December, Friday
The school nativity play. All the fathers had brought camcorders along, and videoed the whole thing, on the off-chance that someone else's child would hurt itself and they could sell the video to *You've Been Framed*. But all went without serious mishap. The Year 1 children were lowly cattle,

asses, sheep and, for some reason, rabbits. There were the Children of All Nations in national costume (apparently the English national costume is the uniform of the Grenadier Guards), plus the usual shepherds wearing tea towels, and three kings with fruit gums stuck on their crowns. And both the boys had insisted on being the star, so the whole procession followed them until they came to rest over the stable where the baby lay, a charming tableau only slightly marred by the boys jostling for centre stage, and the Virgin picking her nose.

Miss Jolly came up to me after the service, a little wet-eyed, and said how nice it would be if I could go in next term and take assembly once a week, maybe looking at Jesus' parables or his healing miracles. I said I'd be delighted.

In the evening, the Bowls Club held their annual carol service in church, with mulled wine and mince pies afterwards. Good to hear all the old favourites again.

8th December, Saturday
Behind the door in the Advent calendar was a moustache, or possibly two slugs saying hello. I looked on the back, to see where it was printed, and what strange foreign culture has such an odd conception of our faith, and all was immediately explained. It was printed in Liverpool. The boys have written to Father Christmas, and asked me whether God tells Father Christmas what to do, or

Father Christmas is God's boss. I told them God is boss of everyone, even Father Christmas, and they looked a bit crestfallen. I asked why, and they said, 'All that writing, and we *still* have to pray.'

9th December, Second Sunday of Advent

The sidesmen have perfected a drill, instructing the congregation where the emergency exits are, how to put on a life jacket, and what to do if oxygen masks fall from the roof. This last is quite improbable – we're more likely to get a fall of manna than oxygen masks, but the sidesmen make the whole thing look like liturgical dance. And we can light the Advent wreath without fear.

Preached on John the Baptist, who once called his congregation a brood of vipers. I don't think I could get away with that, and I'm not about to try. Opened the ninth door of my Advent calendar. Whatever the symbolism of a pair of pants is, I'm afraid it's lost on me.

10th December, Monday

Probably the last day off I'll get this side of Christmas. I had the feeling the whole day that there was something I ought to have been doing. But I soon shook it off, and did a jumbo crossword. Hilary came back from her Caiaphas class (it's like Pilates, but religious), and asked if I'd been shopping. I denied it indignantly.

11th December, Tuesday

Chapter meeting. Apologies from poor old Wilkins, who is in hospital after a bizarre meditation accident, sustained just after last month's meeting. If the rumours are to be believed, he may never uncross his legs again. And as his curate saw him into the ambulance, promising to look after things until he was well, Wilkins waved everything he was still capable of waving, shouting 'No! No!' and demanded to be released. We listened to this account, and spent a few moments in silent reflection. There followed a demonstration of Dressing your Crib Figures. Fascinating stuff, even if the chap doing it called everyone 'dear', and so wet he probably had tadpoles instead of nits. But I was intrigued by the idea of having the shepherds in Barbour jackets, and having the wise men bring Game Boys.

Home to find Hilary and the boys have gone off with Terry Hopkins the photocopier man, leaving a cottage pie in the oven, and no news of where they are. I'm devastated. With all the trouble the photocopier has been over the last six months, and all the carol sheets to do, I don't know what will happen if anything else goes wrong.

December

The Darts Club held their annual carol service in church, with mulled wine and mince pies afterwards. Good to hear all the old favourites again.

12th December, Wednesday
Ate the rest of the cottage pie, so tomorrow I must fend for myself and explore the freezer. No word from Hilary. I'm torn between putting on a brave face and not letting the parish know of my plight, and putting a postcard in the post office window.

The Tennis Club held their annual carol service in church, with mulled wine and mince pies afterwards. It was good to hear all the old favourites again.

13th December, Thursday
Called the Insomnia Society and told them I had leprosy, and couldn't come to the awards lunch. How could I tell them the truth, that without the woman I love by my side, there would be no joy in it at all? The chap on the phone said not to worry, it's usually an archdeacon who wins anyway. Even my food has become insipid to me. Ate fish fingers, which were totally tasteless, not like the way Hilary would have done them. And then I retrieved the packet from the bin, and read it, and it said they were potato croquettes, which are just like tasteless fish fingers because they don't have any fish in them.

The Allotment Holders Association held their annual carol service in church, with mulled wine and mince pies afterwards. I was tempted to send the Potato Most Like the Vicar instead, but thought better of it. And it was good to hear all the old favourites again.

14th December, Friday

Hilary and the boys are back! It seems Terry Hopkins is a total fraud. He isn't a photocopier repair man at all. His real name is Keith something, and he's the lead guitarist in a rock band, resting between stadium tours, a pathetic man who has invented a more exciting persona for himself to get off with women. Hilary confessed tearfully to being dazzled by the glamour, and the aura of mystery, and to being bowled over by his arcane skills, but then she became suspicious when she found his walls covered with gold discs, and a room full of Fender Stratocasters. And it seems he learned a little about photocopiers by watching office-based sitcoms on TV, and made the rest up. Apparently there is no such thing as a trammelling chute.

15th December, Saturday

Opened five windows on my Advent calendar all at once. Somehow, over the last few days, I didn't have the enthusiasm. But at last, some signs of proper festivity – a sock, a candle, some holly, a sprig of mistletoe and, for some reason, a frog.

December

I found the boys giggling in their room and asked them what was so amusing. They said that while they were at Uncle Keith's house, they ripped off his stash. I couldn't help smiling, and hoping it made his eyes water, but as far as I remember, he was clean shaven. Uncle Keith, indeed.

Hilary and I had a thorough heart-to-heart, and it isn't just that I feel I have a duty to forgive her, but I actually want to. And in any case, the best part of breaking up is when you're making up, as the Book of Proverbs says, or if it doesn't it ought to.

16th December, Third Sunday of Advent
Dreadful accident in the aisle, as the crucifer decided on the spur of the moment to genuflect, Adrian somersaulted over him, and the choir piled up on top. The air was thick with flying cassock-buttons and the sound of cotta-seams parting. But a quick roll-call showed nobody was missing, although little Ronnie Stebbings had to be prised out of the heating grating with a Swiss Army knife. The injured were taken away for treatment, and the service continued. Mrs Hopkins came up to me afterwards, and said, 'I hope you realize, Vicar, nothing will get those skid marks out of the carpet.'

17th December, Monday
The church Christmas tree arrived, dropped off a lorry at the bottom of the vicarage drive, so I

couldn't ignore it, but had to drag it up, and into the church. It is our annual gift from the estate that owns most of the land around Cheeving that used to be glebe. The driver said it was a genuine Norway Spruce, and I believe him, because no sooner had I pulled it into the church than a whole lot of lemmings scurried out of it, dashed across the aisle, and leapt into the font.

18th December, Tuesday

Answered the door to find Jason Orrell standing next to an enormous bust, which on closer examination proved be have a pretty blonde girl behind it. When they had been manoeuvred into the study, and I'd straightened the pictures on the walls, Jason said, 'We want to talk about getting married, Vicar', and he seemed so embarrassed I realized he was serious. Next Easter will be the time, and I guess the father of every girl in the village will heave a sigh of relief. The girl's chest blocked out the light while I filled in the form for calling the banns. Jason was reluctant to tell me his middle name, but when I told him I didn't have to read it out loud, he finally admitted that it's Peregrine, which will give me a hold over him against his future good behaviour. I thought the blonde girl with the enormous frontage said she was called Melanie. But she spelt it out for me, M-e-l-o-n-y. 'That's unusual', I said, and she said, 'It means "like melons".' A nice girl. I can see why Jason likes her.

The Bible study group looked at Malachi, very appropriate for Advent. We all thanked Mrs Jellicle for her hospitality over the past year, and she suddenly said, 'That reminds me! Would anyone like a mince pie?'

19th December, Wednesday
Peregrine! Jason Peregrine Orrell!

20th December, Thursday
Cups of tea: 8
Our Fathers: 6
People saying, 'Coming up to your busy time, Vicar': 387

21st December, Friday
I have that wonderful feeling of complacency that comes from having Christmas under control. All the service sheets are done, everybody knows what lessons they're reading and when they're reading them, oranges for Christingles have been ordered, ditto Jelly Tots. Sermons have been written. I can just enjoy the forthcoming festival in peace.

22nd December, Saturday
Christmas presents! I haven't bought anybody any Christmas presents and it's Saturday night and tomorrow is Sunday and then it's Christmas Eve and the shops will be full of thoughtless idiots who left their shopping until the last minute. And I don't even know what anybody wants.

23rd December, Fourth Sunday of Advent
Hilary has bailed me out yet again because she has been buying Christmas presents since October. 'But what about you?' I asked. 'I haven't even bought you anything.' Hilary pointed to a small parcel nestling almost unnoticed with the rest. 'Yes you have,' she said, 'and it will be a lovely surprise.'

I preached on the hymn, 'O come, O come Emmanuel' and explained what all the 'rod of Jesse' and 'key of David' and 'dayspring' images mean. As we've sung it every week for the past month, I thought it was about time.

24th December, Monday, Christmas Eve
House communions all morning, and then I stuck  my head in church to encourage the flower ladies, and get the crib figures out of the vestry cupboard. Hilary's parents arrived, asked me when I was going to get a proper job, kissed the

boys, and then I made them help assembling Christingles. I made the holes in the oranges, Hilary stuck in the candles, her mum wrapped the red ribbon around, and her dad stuck Jelly Tots on little sticks. And we all did our best to stop the boys eating the Jelly Tots, with little success.

Adrian excelled himself at the Christingle service, having made a giant Christingle out of a space-hopper left over from the 1970s, a box of those big fruit jellies, and the remains of the Paschal candle, which he hadn't fixed on firmly enough, which is part of the reason our insurance premium next year will probably be more than our diocesan share.

25th December, Tuesday, Christmas Day

As usual, a lot of drunks straight out of the Temporary Sign turned up at the midnight service, some of them so far gone they could hardly get into their choir robes. But the church was full, and the atmosphere at last made me feel festive. Home to find the boys had left Santa a glass of sherry and a mince pie, so I accepted them on his behalf. Barely an hour in bed when the boys rushed in, demanding to open their presents. Which they did, which meant nobody got any sleep afterwards. And they insisted I open their present for me, which was a Harry Potter Lego set, which they kindly offered to put together for me, and I was too tired to protest.

Good services throughout the morning, with the

choir singing like angels, and my arm quite sore from all the handshakes and Happy Christmases.

I had some touching gifts from parishioners. Several people gave me one of those little boxes with seashells glued all over them. Everybody was delighted with the presents I had given them, and Hilary was absolutely delighted with the necklace and earrings I had bought her. Even her father admired them, and said, 'I thought you parsons were supposed to be hard up.'

Lunch was excellent. Hilary had pulled out all the stops, and then I think I might have nodded off.

26th December, Wednesday, St Stephen's Day, Boxing Day, Second Day of Christmas
I remember the year I tried to have a St Stephen's Day service, and nobody came because they were all celebrating in their own way, by getting stoned.

Hilary's parents went home, and she turned down their offer to go with them. 'Don't forget,' her dad shouted as the car gathered speed down the drive, 'Our door is always open!'

27th December, Thursday
I'm supposed to have all this week off, but I never feel I can relax when there's a Sunday to look forward to. And there are always more people I want to visit than there is time to visit them. But it was a good day for sherry and mince pies, and by lunch time I was too full of both to be much use to

anybody. So in the afternoon, we sat and played the boys' new game, which Hilary's parents gave them for Christmas. It has apparently been scientifically designed to make dads look like complete twits, and did it very well.

28th December, Friday
Harry Parry called to see me, with a smile on his face you could have posted letters in. He said, 'You remember that Easter egg at the bazaar?' And I admitted I did, and asked if anyone bought it. 'No,' he said, 'I took it to London.' 'London?' I said. 'Yes, London,' he said, 'Just this side of Ilford.' Then he got to the point, and told me that he'd taken the egg to Chrisseby's the auctioneers, and they had sold it, and he showed me the cheque made out to St Gargoyle's PCC, and if I'd been sitting down I'd have fallen off my chair, but as I was standing up, I settled for falling over. Harry assured me this wasn't a joke, offered to pinch me to prove I wasn't dreaming and said, 'You know what this means, Vicar?' And I said yes, it means I can tell Don Capelletti he won't have to kidnap the boys after all, and someone in London has more money than sense, God bless them.

29th December, Saturday
I spent the best part of two hours writing a sermon

for tomorrow, and then Hilary pointed out that it's the big carol service, and if I preach, a lot of people are going to be seriously disappointed. I said for all she knew, it might be the high spot of their holiday, and Hilary said, 'Hah!' like she does. It's so good to know that my wife hasn't put me on a pedestal, and keeps me from the sin of pride. Come to think of it, she keeps me from the sins of gluttony, lust and sloth as well.

30th December, First Sunday of Christmas
Never mind the coffee and Rich Tea biscuits, we had sausage rolls, mince pies and mulled wine after the service, an ancient custom we started last year. And when the Colonel asked, with his mouth full, 'Who's paying for this?' I just topped him up and winked at Harry, and when Mrs Hopkins looked at the crumbs and asked who was clearing up, I promised to buy her a new vacuum cleaner. 'One of those with cheeky eyes and a bowler hat?' she asked. 'If that's what you would like,' I said, 'you shall have it.'

In among the crowds, I found Jason Orrell and Melony. Jason said, a bit self-consciously, 'I really enjoyed that, Vicar. Maybe we'll come again next week.' I said they were welcome any time, and made a mental note to look out for flying pigs.

31st December, Monday, New Year's Eve
We stayed up to see the New Year in. Hilary said what a strange year it had been, and I thought

about it, and it strikes me it has been, if anything, less eventful than last year. I didn't win the Lottery (but then I never bought a ticket) and the boys noticeably failed to sprout wings, although I asked them over the turkey risotto whether they were going to make any New Year resolutions. They both said, 'Yes. To be good.' So even more reason to beware the flying pigs. But even if this year has been just like any other, there's always next year, and who knows? Something momentous might happen.